PLAIN TALK
on Christian Doctrine

A Pastor Looks at the
Westminster Shorter Catechism

by
GORDON K. REED

PLAIN TALK
on Christian Doctrine

By Gordon Kenworthy Reed

Copyright ©2019 by Tanglewood Publishing

978-0-9972490-9-5

All rights reserved. No part of this book may be reproduced In any form without written permission from

Tanglewood Publishing
tanglewoodpublishing.org
601-924-5020

Book Design and Layout by Mieke Moller
Cover Design by Christy Rodriguez

Printed in the United States of America

INTRODUCTION

Generations of Christians have been brought up memorizing the Shorter Catechism, but the Catechism is now, unfortunately, a hidden treasure to many. Countless churches in which it once was a central component of Christian education now ignore it, and modern educational methods discount memorization of anything. But despite it all, the Catechism will amply repay anyone who will devote the time to study it. That's one reason I am delighted to commend to you this fine book on the Shorter Catechism. Allow me to explain why I believe the Catechism is important and why Gordon Reed's popular commentary on it will prove so helpful.

What's so good about the Shorter Catechism? Why should we still study it? Well, there are many good answers to those questions. Here are a few. First, the Catechism is biblical! It is not just that there are Scripture references attached to every question, but rather that the answer to each question is thoroughly biblical. Its content is drawn from the teaching of the Holy Bible. The men who wrote the Catechism took a vow not to include anything that they could not demonstrate from Scripture. In a day and age in which the Bible's teaching and contents are unfamiliar to many churchgoing Christians, the Shorter Catechism provides sound biblical answers to important theological and practical questions.

Second, the Catechism makes a practical contribution to Christian faith and life. Most people of our day have decided that life (and even Christian ministry) should be carried out pragmatically rather than theologically. In other words, we ask "what works?" (or worse, "what works for me?") rather than "what does God tell us to do in His Word?" This salad bar-style approach to Christian belief and practice panders to the worst sort of individualism. The Catechism, thankfully, offers us a corrective: a practical pattern of belief and life that is based on Biblical principles.

Third, the Catechism has made a historical contribution to Christian faith and life. *The Westminster Confession and Catechisms* (so called because they were written by a group of ministers and elders at Westminster Abbey in London) have served for over three centuries as the basic doctrinal formulary for Presbyterianism, but they have also been influential in the Baptist (e.g., via the Second London Confession of 1689, adopted as the Philadelphia Confession in 1742) and Congregational (e.g., via the Savoy Declaration of 1658) traditions. But of all the things that the Westminster Assembly wrote, the Catechism has been the most widely used. This, in and of itself, is a good reason why we ought to study it.

Fourth, the Catechism makes an important contribution to our doctrinal discernment. Knowledge and appreciation of the Shorter Catechism can serve to inoculate us against the false teachings and faddish Christianity of our own age. "Reading old books," C.S. Lewis once said, keeps "the clean sea breeze of the centuries blowing through our minds" so that we are not so prone to modern errors. In an era where many Christians are blown about by "every wind of doctrine," the biblical sanity of the Catechism will prove a real help.

Fifth, the Catechism makes an important contribution to doctrinal maturity in the Christian faith and life. The saving knowledge of God is essential to Christian living. This entails knowing God personally and learning about Him through His word. Because of this, all Christians are called to be theologians – the question is whether we are going to be good ones or bad ones! – and that is where study of the Catechism comes in.

The mastering of the Catechism will provide the Christian with a wholesome and comprehensive grasp of biblical truth. That truth, in turn, is crucial for Christian living, because what we believe affects how we live. Bad theology leads to bad practice. As Stephen Charnock said so long ago: "It is impossible to honor God as we ought, unless we know Him as He is." The study of the Catechism will give us a surer knowledge of God as He has revealed Himself in the Scripture.

Sixth, the Catechism makes a wonderful contribution to the

cultivation of "Christian Piety" or "Heart Religion." The devotional value of the Shorter Catechism should not be overlooked. There is much, indeed, to feed our souls that we can learn from the Catechism. The Catechism provides for us both a profound, reverent, affectionate exposition of the doctrines of the Bible and a worthy model of the function of truth in the pursuit of godliness. There is nothing cold and academic about the Catechism; rather we find here a warm, evangelical expression of the Christian faith. This is nowhere more evident than in the very first question and answer of the Catechism: *What is the chief end of man? A. Man's chief end is to glorify God, and to enjoy him forever.* (I Corinthians 10:31 and Psalm 73:25-26). You can't get more basic or practical than this. What is the meaning of life? What is our purpose in life? What are we here for? If you get the answer to this question wrong, everything else will go wrong. To glorify God is to know him and obey him, according to his word. To enjoy him is to seek him as our greatest good and our greatest desire. Nothing cold or academic about that! For all those reasons (and more) you ought to avail yourself of the Catechism. Furthermore, you will find this book a helpful, practical, pastoral, and devotional introduction and guide to the Catechism.

Gordon Reed is a skillful writer and gifted preacher, with years of pastoral experience. He brings a lifetime of experience to this exposition of the Catechism. He not only knows the theology of the Catechism, he lives it. He is such a good popular communicator that he will make difficult topics seem more accessible (you will see his warmth and sense of humor page after page), and he is such a good theologian that he will challenge and stimulate you with his biblical insights. (He never ceases to amaze me with his ability to summarize an important truth in a single simple sentence.) For preachers and teachers, he not only supplies an excellent explanation of each question of the Catechism, but he offers numerous helpful illustrations and applications of these biblical truths. For students of Scripture, young and old, he clearly explains Bible doctrine in an enjoyable and engaging way. Thus, this volume will helpfully serve both as a devotional help and as a teaching aid.

May the Lord of heaven bless you, dear reader, as you read

and meditate upon the truth of his word as it is so clearly set forth in this study of the Shorter Catechism.

J. Ligon Duncan, III, PhD

Chancellor & CEO of Reformed Theological Seminary and the John E. Richards Professor of Systematic and Historical Theology. He served as Senior Minister of the historic First Presbyterian Church (1837) in Jackson, Miss. for 17 years (1996-2013).

Question #1: *What is the chief end of man?*

Answer: *Man's chief end is to glorify God, and to enjoy Him forever.*

It has been said, and it is probably true, that few people ever ask the truly important questions in life. The three most frequently asked questions in America are: (1) How can I lose weight? (2) Where can I park my car? (3) Who won the ball game? Here in the first question of the catechism, we are faced with life's most important question, *What is the chief end of man?* Another way of asking the same question might be, *Who am I?* or *Why am I here?* or *What is the meaning of my life?*

This question in the catechism speaks to such things as reality and purpose. Are these things important for you? How long has it been since you gave serious thought to the meaning and purpose of your life?

Notice that the catechism asks what is the *chief* end of man. By this word, recognition is given to those many lesser purposes which may occupy our thoughts and efforts. These things may be of greater or lesser importance in relation to each other, and some are of considerable importance indeed. Where we live and what career we pursue are important matters to consider. The choice of one's life-mate is far more important than career or location. However, the catechism (and the Bible) recognize that there is one great purpose which overshadows all others, and for which we have been created and redeemed. Just to know that there is ultimate purpose and meaning to life is both exciting and comforting. To have one great purpose also gives added significance to all other purposes and goals. This means that all we do – working, planning, education, recreation, family life, and even eating and sleeping, have meaning which flows from the one great purpose. That purpose centers in God and our relationship to Him. The meaning of our existence depends upon this. Our chief end above all lesser ones is to glorify God and to enjoy Him forever. This means that we must first know Him as He reveals Himself to us. It means to acknowledge His existence and

His sovereignty. We are His people and the sheep of His pasture. To glorify God is to reflect His image and character, which may only be done by those who have been drawn to Him by irresistible grace and saving love in Christ Jesus. To glorify God is to honor Him by faith and obedience.

But to fulfill our purpose we must also enjoy Him. In fact, it would be impossible to glorify Him unless we do enjoy Him. This is a warm and glowing word. It is a word to gladden our hearts, for it is a love word. Joy and love walk hand in hand, and loving Him who first loved us is pure and holy joy. It is for this we were created and redeemed. It is for this we live, for unless we know, glorify, enjoy, and love Him, we do not really live at all; we merely exist.

The final word in this formula for true living is *forever*. The answer is incomplete without it. It is the *foreverness* of our relationship to God that brings the greatest joy and enables us to truly glorify Him. *Forever* means heaven. It means a new heaven and a new earth, a restored and perfected creation. The last two chapters in the Bible, Revelation 20 and 21, give us a glimpse of what *forever* really means. Just a glimpse is more glorious than our minds can comprehend. But to know that we shall one day live in the midst of that wonder is truly glory and joy forever.

Question #2: *What rule hath God given to direct us how we may glorify and enjoy Him?*

Answer: *The Word of God, which is contained in the Scriptures of the Old and New Testaments, is the only rule to direct us how we may glorify and enjoy Him.*

The obvious truth that life centers in and derives its meaning from our relationship to God has led mankind on a frantic search for God from the earliest days until now. Tragically, that quest has never succeeded and is always doomed to failure. In fact, this quest has led mankind further and further away from God and has left us frustrated at every turn. Does this mean we may never know the true God? Does this mean we will never know our true meaning nor achieve our destiny? No, there is a way – God's way – by which we may know how to glorify and enjoy our Creator-Father. God has come in search of us that we might learn of Him and that in His search for us, we may find Him.

How and where do we learn to know, glorify, and enjoy Him forever? There are many attempted answers to this question, but there is only one that is true and right: *In the Bible alone.* The ability to know God depends directly upon this truth. All other avenues lead to error and darkness, and in the end, they lead to death and separation from God forever. The latter part of the first chapter of Romans comments on the futility of fallen creatures' search for the true Creator. It is a depressing catalog of failure and futility.

However, God has revealed Himself. He has made it possible even for little children to know Him and to find salvation and life by that true knowledge. Isn't it wonderful to know that God has given us a book which enables us to know Him? The Bible is God's autobiography. He is the author and He is the subject. The Bible teaches many things. It tells us of the creation of the universe and the origin of life. It talks about who we are and how we came to be. It reveals the story of evil and how we became sinners. It traces the history of the human race in broad strokes and focuses on the lives of individual people who lived on earth long ago. These things and many more are found in the Bible, but above all things, events, and people, the Bible reveals God – the one true and living God – Father, Son, and Holy Spirit. Because the Bible alone reveals Him, it is also the only rule (guide) to direct us how we may glorify and enjoy Him.

A popular song years ago made the proud boast, *I did it my way.* The Christian knows the important thing is to do it God's way. What we must never forget is that God's way may be found only in God's book, the Bible.

The Bible is a most remarkable book! God used many different people to write His book. These people lived in different times and circumstances. They wrote in many different styles and found themselves in many different circumstances. They all had one thing in common. They were channels through whom God, the Holy Spirit, revealed the Living Word. Although written in the languages of long ago, the Bible has been translated into many languages all over the world and has lost nothing in the translation! The Bible you hold in your hand and read with your eyes or hear with your ears is God's Holy Word. Let the scholars debate which translation is the best one. (They will disagree.) Ask your pastor to recommend a good translation and read it as God's Word, for this is what it is. As you read it, the Holy Spirit will open your mind and heart and you will learn from this book how you may glorify and enjoy God.

Question #3: *What do the Scriptures principally teach?*

Answer: *The Scriptures principally teach, what man is to believe concerning God, and what duty God requires of man.*

The Bible is God's Word. That Word is all-sufficient for all believers. The third question of the Shorter Catechism focuses on the central truths of Scripture. The key word here is *what* do the Scriptures principally teach. The Bible is mainly concerned with two matters: doctrine and duty, faith and life. It touches on many other things. It supplies the foundation on which all truth rests and serves as glasses through which we may understand the truth that comes to us through nature or other avenues. By God's grace, there is much truth available to our minds for our good. But it must be understood in light of God's special revelation, the Bible.

Before looking at those matters the Bible principally teaches, let us say that wherever the Bible speaks, it speaks truth. When it speaks in the area of human nature, history, or the physical sciences, it speaks truth and is the only infallible interpreter of all other truth in these areas. When human learning and the teaching of Scripture appears to be in conflict, there are only two possibilities. Either human learning is in error or we have misunderstood Scripture.

Now what of the major concerns of Scripture? First of all, the Bible teaches truth about God. It tells us what we must believe about Him and about ourselves. All human efforts to discover who God is have failed to give a clear and saving knowledge of the great Creator-God. All human concepts fall short of the true God and dishonor Him. This is true of the most primitive ideas derived from nature and of the most sophisticated concepts drawn from philosophical reasoning. Only in the Bible do we meet the true and living eternal God. In its pages alone do we see His true character and glorious nature, His sovereignty, His holiness, and His grace. Never could nature or the mind of man discover the wonder of His love and saving power. It is only in the Bible we learn that *God so loved the world, that he gave His only begotten Son, that whosoever believeth in Him should not perish, but have everlasting life.* Only in the Bible can we find such lofty concepts of God as are revealed in Isaiah 40.

The Bible also reveals that this God requires certain duty from us. It comes as a surprise to the modern Christian to discover that God requires anything! We have become so accustomed to a gospel that speaks only of what God gives us that we tend to forget He also requires from us loving obedience to His commands. *He has shown you, O man, what is good and what does the Lord require of you but to do justly, and to love mercy, and to walk humbly with thy God?* This verse from Micah is a beautiful, simple summary of all the Scripture teaches about our duty to God. The Christian who wants to please and honor, to glorify and enjoy God forever will carefully search the Scriptures of both Old and New Testaments to discover the duty we owe Him, and in so doing will come to know that we must love the Lord our God with all our hearts, mind, and strength, and our neighbor as ourselves.

The Bible tells us that God is infinite and eternal. That means He has always been and that He is everywhere. We cannot possibly know everything about God. We only know what He Himself shows us, and that is enough for our salvation. He is unchangeable. We may always depend upon God. Since He is absolutely perfect in every way, He has never changed nor will He. Something perfect cannot change for the better. The God who created the world is the God who sent His Son to die for sinners. God is not only infinite, eternal, and unchangeable in His being, He is all these things in all His attributes. His wisdom, power, holiness, justice, goodness, and truth are all forever and forever perfect and complete. He will always be these things and you may know Him, trust Him, and love Him in complete confidence.

Question #4: *What is God?*

Answer: *God is a Spirit, infinite, eternal, and unchangeable in his being, wisdom, power, holiness, justice, goodness, and truth.*

What a question! Who and what is God? Dr. J.B. Green says in his *Harmony of the Westminster Standards*, "As a definition of undefinable deity, the Shorter Catechism is unexcelled, unequaled by any word of man." That is high praise, but well-deserved. This question was a major concern of those saints at Westminster who wrote the Confession and the Catechism. It is said that after many long hours of study and discussion, a prayer was offered to God for help in answering this most difficult of all questions. The prayer began, "Oh God, thou who art spirit, infinite, eternal, and unchangeable in thy being, wisdom, power, holiness, justice, goodness, and truth…" God answered the prayer for help by giving to those who prayed the words of the prayer itself.

It was Jesus who said, "God is Spirit…" This simply means that God exists forever and always as a Spirit. He does not have a body like man, yet He knows, sees, speaks and hears and loves and rejoices.

The invisible Spirit God has no body like man, but He has a character and personality. The Bible tells us that He is infinite and eternal. That means He has always existed and that He is everywhere. We cannot possibly know everything about God. We only know what He Himself shows us, and that is enough for our salvation. He tells us that He is unchangeable. We may always depend upon God. Since He is absolutely perfect in every way, He has never changed nor will He. When something is perfect, it cannot change. The God who created the world is the God who sent His Son to die for sinners.

God is not only infinite, eternal, and unchangeable in His being, He is all these things in all of His attributes. His wisdom, His power, His holiness, His justice, His goodness, and His truth are all forever and forever perfect and complete. He will always be all these things, and you may know Him, trust Him, and love Him in complete confidence. He will never change.

As a little child, I had the idea that my parents would always be there for me, that they would always be strong and healthy and wise and provide all my needs. As I grew older, so did they, and eventually they became old and feeble and dependent on others. Our great heavenly Father, who is perfect in Himself and in all aspects of His character, always will be perfect, and through His son Jesus Christ we may live in His house forever.

Question #5: *Are there more gods than one?*

Answer: *There is but one only, the living and true God.*

After asking the question, "What is God?" next comes the question, "Is He alone or are there more Gods than one?" The simple affirmation is expected, but it is far more profound and far more important than it may appear at first glance. Although the ancient forms of polytheism may no longer be evident, at least as they once appeared, yet the basic sin is still very much with us and there in many forms.

The one living and true God is the God who meets us in the Bible. He is the God and Father of our Lord Jesus Christ. The Muslim claims to have the sole knowledge of God, whom he calls Allah. He claims this God may only be known through his prophet Mohammed. We must never fall into the trap of thinking this is the same God we worship, but by another name. Many modern cults claim that the God they teach is the God of the Bible, but then they add their own ideas and subtract from the teachings of the Bible. Again we must recognize that their god is not the God of the Bible, nor the God our Lord Jesus came to reveal. So when those nicely dressed young men who are missionaries for the Mormon church come to your door, just remember they do not represent the one living and true God. Their god is not the God and Father of our Lord Jesus Christ.

The same thing is true of those who claim to be Jehovah's Witnesses. Though they may claim to be a branch of the Christian church, they are not. They are false witnesses.

False gods are not limited to pagan superstitions nor cultic misrepresentations. They exist in our sophisticated culture, too. These are the gods of materialism and self-indulgence, the gods of sex and drugs. In the Western world, atheism in the form of secular humanism has almost become the official religion of many nations, including the United States, and once Christian nations such as Holland and Sweden. Furthermore, whatever claims first place in our lives becomes our god. Yet these things are not gods, but vain imaginations and delusions.

There is but one only, the living and true God who requires of us that we love Him with all our heart, strength, and mind. He is worthy, and He alone, to receive the worship, praise, and adoration of our hearts and lives.

A little child was once asked, "How many gods are there?"

He replied, "There is only one God."

"How do you know this?" he was asked.

"Because there is only room for Him alone, because He fills the whole universe."

Good answer, wise child. There is a beautiful and powerful story in the Old Testament which speaks to this truth. It is the story of Elijah and the prophets of Baal. On the slopes of Mt. Carmel, the man of God challenged the four hundred false prophets to prove the existence and power of their god. In spite of their most frantic efforts they could not, for Baal was but an idol of stone. After their failure, Elijah prayed to the one living and true God. He answered with fire from heaven which consumed the offering and the altar, and burned away the idolatry in the hearts of His people. So as we faithfully serve this same true God and prove by our redeemed lives His power and glory, we join hands with Elijah in the work of God, and lead others to cry out, *The Lord He is God…alone!*

Question #6: *How many persons are there in the Godhead?*

Answer: *There are three persons in the Godhead: the Father, the Son, and the Holy Ghost; and these three are one God, the same in substance, equal in power and glory.*

There is no truth concerning God that is not relevant and urgent in the life of the believer. Everything He chooses to tell us about Himself has direct bearing on who we are and what we must know and believe about Him. This is most certainly true of the doctrine of the Trinity. Let's try to see how this truth applies to our salvation and our experience as Christians.

We begin in eternity, before the world was created. In the covenant of redemption, God, the Father, elected to Himself a people chosen before the foundation of the earth to be His own. God, the Son, in perfect unity and harmony with the Father's will, covenanted to win their salvation by His incarnation and atonement. God, the Holy Ghost, covenanted to apply both the electing grace of the Father and the atoning grace of the Son to each individual among the elect. Thus, the three persons of the Godhead are directly and immediately involved in our salvation.

Prayer is one of the most precious gifts to the elect. It is our link with heaven, our lifeline to God. In prayer we come before the Father and address Him. Jesus taught us about prayer when He said, *After this manner therefore pray ye: Our Father who art in heaven…* Furthermore, the Lord Jesus told us that we are to come before the

Father in His (Jesus') name. It is only through our Lord Jesus Christ that we may come to the Father. The good news is that we may come to the Father, and that His Son gives us free access into the holy presence.

The Spirit's role in prayer is equally important. Even though we do not know how to pray as we ought, the blessed Spirit makes intercession for us *with groanings which cannot be uttered*. The Spirit convicts of sin, and at the same time assures us and encourages us to confess our sins in prayer to the Father by the name and blood of His Son. The normal pattern of prayer, then, is to come to the Father, through the Son, by the Holy Spirit.

Christian family life reflects the pattern of the Trinity. In the creation of our first parents, Adam and Eve, the Bible tells us: *So God created man in His own image, in the image of God created He him: male and female created He them.* So ideally in Christian marriage there is intended to be a oneness of heart and purpose, intimate love and abiding peace and harmony. Yet there is distinction and respect of persons, just as there are distinct persons within the Godhead. The Son is eternally begotten of the Father, and the Spirit proceeds from the Father and the Son. So, in God's plan for Christian marriage the parents are to beget children with whom they share nature and loving relationship.

Yes, the doctrine of the Trinity lies at the very heart of all Christian theology, and it underlies all Christian experience. It is an essential doctrine, and it is also a very precious truth. Be warned, beloved, any person or any system which does not clearly and forthrightly proclaim the Biblical doctrine of the Trinity is to be rejected and avoided. Let God be God, and let Him tell us in His word of His glorious triune nature.

Question #7: *What are the decrees of God?*

Answer: *The decrees of God are, his eternal purpose, according to the counsel of his will, whereby, for his own glory, he hath foreordained whatsoever comes to pass.*

The expression *the decrees of God* has a strange and even ominous sound for many people. This is unfortunate and need not be so. The problem is that we associate the word decree with human authority, and even human despotism. God's decrees are entirely different from that. To understand this truth which the catechism presents, you must begin with the nature and character of God. In our earlier studies we discovered that God who is spirit is absolutely perfect in His being and in all His glorious attributes. He is the God of wisdom, power, holiness, justice, goodness, and truth. Apart from this understanding of God, the idea of His decrees might be frightening indeed. However, because of God's character we may rejoice in the concept and praise Him with great joy for His decrees.

Our God has an eternal purpose. This purpose is rooted in His own nature. He has a plan for all His creation. Everything He does, all His great and gracious acts, flows from this purpose. His purpose is consistent with His character. In His wisdom He has decreed that we must act as responsible moral beings, accountable to Him for our behavior. However, the ultimate outcome does not rest upon man's free will and human decisions and choices. The plan of the ages was not the product of a committee! The book of Job raises the question, *With whom did He (God) take counsel?* It also answers that question with a resounding, *No one!*

What does it mean to say that God foreordained whatsoever comes to pass? Simply that God is in control. He rules and overrules in all things. There is not one atom in this entire universe out of His control. Not a sparrow falls to the ground without the Father. He has numbered the hairs of your head and the stars in the heavens. Why has God doe this? Why has He foreordained all things which come to pass? His is the highest and purest motive of all. For His own glory He has decreed all things. Again let it be said that His purpose is rooted in His character. There can be no higher motive than complete perfection.

Just a few swift glances at Scripture will show that this is not a new doctrine. It is not something the Westminster Divines dreamed up. It is a Biblical doctrine. One might say it is the Biblical doctrine of God. It is taught from the first to the last. It meets us in the first two chapters of Genesis in the account of creation. Nothing could be more obvious than to say that creation was according to a plan. As the biblical record tells the story of creation, it reveals an orderly and well-planned world. This truth is also written into the very fabric of creation itself. Because God foreordains whatsoever comes to pass, we may observe His handiwork and see both purpose and plan in all His creation.

In God's covenant with Adam, there is a high and holy purpose revealed. This purpose was written into the soul of Adam and Eve. It was to be their guide and motive for living. It held the promise of grace and glory for the whole human race. Even in the fall God's purpose was not frustrated, but rather fulfilled. With our finite minds, we may never be able to understand this, but we may trust the infinite mind of God, who works all things according to the counsel of His own will, ruling and overruling in all things.

The same is true in the story of Noah. God's plan included both judgment and mercy: judgment on the unbelieving world, mercy upon the man who found favor with God and who lived the life of faith and obedience. There are many, many prophecies in the Old Testament about the coming Messiah. How was this possible? Only because it was a part of God's plan and purpose which He revealed to the prophets. The New Testament adds its testimony to this doctrine. The book of Ephesians is one great example. In chapter 1, Paul tells us that God's gracious decrees mean that we have every spiritual blessing in Christ. We are chosen in Him before the foundation of the world. This choice of love results in our adoption into His family. By this we are assured that we are heirs of God and joint-heirs of Christ. Now does the expression *the decrees of God* sound ominous? Far from it. It is a blessed word, a sweet and lovely sound in the believer's ear and heart.

Question #8: *How doth God execute his decrees?*

Answer: *God executeth his decrees in the works of creation and providence.*

What good is a plan or even a purpose if you lack the ability to carry out or execute that plan? Our God has decreed whatsoever comes to pass, and He is actively at work to carry out His decrees. This is a very important truth to understand. There are those who would think of God as some sort of impersonal force or first cause who is not directly involved in His creation. The Deists thought of God as simply winding up the universe and then letting it run under its own power. This is not the God of the Bible. God executes His own decrees. It is true that He uses secondary causes and He uses people to carry out His purposes, but it is God who executes His decrees by whatever means.

Many years ago (how many I refuse to say on the grounds it might tend to date me) our football coach used to say something like this: "Boys, I have a good game plan, but it will only win the game for us if you execute the plays." That is something of what we mean when we say that God not only purposes and plans, but He is constantly at work to carry through and carry out His plan.

Several years ago, a couple visited my study to ask for help in saving their marriage, which was about to come to a tragic and needless end. After a few counseling sessions, it became clear that one of their major problems was simply a lack of any understanding of an organized pattern of living. They had no family schedule, no budget, no plans for the present or future. I worked with them for some time, developing some organization to their lives. In short, we worked out a "game plan" for their marriage. They both agreed this was needed. They both worked with me to develop a mutually agreeable plan, and verbally committed themselves to it. I felt good about the future for them. However, within a few weeks they were back again with more of the same problems as well as new ones. They had a good plan, but they were unable or unwilling to work out the plan.

What if God was unable or unwilling to execute His decrees? They would have no meaning at all for Him or for us. Fortunately, this is not the case. In fact, the catechism is very specific in answering the question "How doth God execute His decrees?" He executes His decrees in the works of creation and providence. Later we shall see in more detail what these works are, and how they individually serve to execute His decrees. For now, let it be said that God is personally involved in His creation and especially in the lives of His precious elect. He is the fountainhead of life itself. His great work of creation was simply the beginning of the execution of His eternal purpose. God the grand designer became God the great contractor when He began to say, "Let there be…" and it was so.

Upon the completion of this work of creation, after creating man, male and female, in His own image, God immediately began to execute His decrees in the work of providence. This work involved and still involves His provision and care for all His creation, His ordaining and foreordaining all events and circumstances which affect our lives. In the Bible you seldom, if ever, find an expression like "The wind blew" or "It rained." Rather you may read, *God sent a great wind* or *God caused it to rain*. Even when the Scriptures do not specifically say that such things were done by the hand of God, the implication is clearly there.

God is not remote, or even far away. He is ever near and ever at work executing His decrees. What a blessing and comfort to know that it is God who works all things together for good to those who love Him and are called according to His purpose.

———

Question #9:   *What is the work of creation?*

Answer: *The work of creation is, God's making all things of nothing, by the word of His power, in the space of six days, and all very good.*

The whole matter and question of creation has been a major issue for the entire twentieth century and even before. Naturalistic scientists have disputed the Biblical account of creation for many years. This has been especially true since the work of Darwin and his disciples. The capitulation of the believing community to this philosophy of unbelief has been and continues to be one of the major tragedies of modern-day Christianity. This surrender and compromise has not only included liberalism within the church, but a large portion of the evangelical sector as well.

However, in these latter days, God has raised up a band of dedicated scientists who are also Bible-believing Christians. These scholars have taken up the task of presenting the case for scientific creationism. They have called into question the basic assumptions of naturalism and have exposed the folly of theistic evolutionism. Yet their greatest contribution is not their ability to debate the issues scientifically, but rather to call believers back to the statements of Scripture as the foundation for all truth and the starting point for the exploration of the natural world.

When the catechism and the Bible speak of creation, they use the term in a very unique sense. We talk about creating a work of art. In the strictest sense this is not a creation at all, but a forming into other shapes of existing materials. We may talk of an author creating a novel or a poem, but again, this is not really a creation, but a use of things which have existed previously to produce a work of literature. The catechism teaches us that God made all things of nothing. In the book of Hebrews we read these words: *Through faith we understand that the worlds were framed by the word of God, so that things which are seen were not made of things which do appear.* This teaches us that when God created the world, He brought into being things which did not exist before. He did not take primeval ooze and shape it into the world that now is. The Bible is very explicit in telling us that the Lord God spoke the word, and those things described came into being then and there. The Gospel of John reminds us that it was by the eternal Word that all things were made, and that without Him was not anything made that was made.

A word needs to be said concerning the time required for creation. Both the Bible and the catechism make it very plain that it all took place in the space of six days. Since the ascendancy of Darwinian evolutionism in the scientific world, the Church has been frantically explaining to itself and to one and all that the word *day* appears several times in Scripture referring to an era, or period of time. This is true. But where in Scripture does the word *day* appear used in the same explicit, detailed way as seen in Genesis 1? Where in all Scripture does the expression appear: *And there was evening and there was morning, one day*, meaning an era, or an indefinite period of time? While it is not impossible to think of the word day as referring to an indefinite period of time, it is certainly a strained interpretation in the context of Genesis 1.

One final word concerning creation. It was all very good. Of course it was, for it was made by the God who is Himself good, and wise and holy. Of all God's works we may say, "And behold it was very good" (Genesis 1:31).

Question #10: *How did God create man?*

Answer: *God created man, male and female, after his own image, in knowledge, righteousness, and holiness, with dominion over the creatures.*

God created man! This may well be the most significant statement in the entire catechism. It is foundational for every other truth we know concerning mankind. It is absolutely essential to know this and to say this before we ever discuss the doctrines of grace. The Christian faith as a body of revealed truth rests upon this foundation: God created man. The creation of man took place on the sixth day of creation, thus signifying that everything else in the order of creation was in preparation for the grand finale when God created man.

This Biblical truth places us in direct and irreconcilable conflict with the evolutionary myths concerning the beginning of the human race. There is simply no meeting ground for the one who believes that an all-wise, powerful, and holy God created man for His own glory and according to His eternal plan, and those who believe that man is the product of evolutionary chance with no meaning or purpose to his existence. All attempts at reconciliation between these two opposing philosophies end up in unacceptable compromise for the believer.

The catechism notes the Biblical emphasis that both male and female were created in God's image. There are two things which deserve special attention at this point. In light of the present situation in our confused and lost culture, we need to affirm both. First, there is a basic equality between the sexes. Both male and female were created in God's image. The idea that either man or woman is somehow qualitatively superior to the other is not Biblical. The Biblical teaching of spiritual leadership that God has given to the husband and father may be, and often is, distorted into a non-Biblical male chauvinism thinly veiled as the "Reformed view." On the other hand, a radical feminist position which denies the role of headship to the husband and father is off-base as well. The second thing we must affirm is the distinction between the sexes. The Bible repeatedly makes the point that there is a distinction between the sexes, and that distinction is built into the nature of man, both male and female. A clear understanding and affirmation of this Biblical truth would go a long way towards refuting some of the most serious errors gaining acceptance in our society today, such as homosexuality and radical feminism.

There has always been some confusion in the minds of many concerning the image of God in man. Some people think that the image of God in man refers to his physical appearance. This is not at all what is intended by this statement. Nor does it mean that we have the spark of divinity within us as the old liberal position claimed. What it does mean is that there are some things in the nature of man similar to God's nature. Some of the same characteristics found in God are also found in man. Man has the ability to think, to speak, to love, and to have fellowship. He can (in his created state before the fall) discern good from evil. He can act according to a plan and a purpose. All these things are found to perfection in God's nature, but only to a degree in man. The eternal God created man with an immortal soul.

One of the aspects of God's image in man is that of dominion. Man was created with both the ability and the mandate to rule over creation as God's steward. This dominion was not absolute, nor was it autocratic in the usual sense. It was a sacred trust, an internship of training for a future charge of far greater proportions. As Christians we will one day be restored to that position of dominion. We are destined to be heirs of God and joint heirs with Christ. The saints will judge the world and reign with Christ throughout all eternity.

Question #11: *What are God's works of providence?*

Answer: *God's works of providence are, his most holy, wise, and powerful preserving and governing all his creatures, and all their actions.*

Next to the doctrines of predestination and election, this doctrine is the most difficult of all to understand or for human minds and reason to accept. Next to the doctrines of election and predestination, it is the most precious of all Biblical truths. The Shorter Catechism's answer to this question is a brief, but brilliant, summary of an entire chapter in the Confession of Faith, and two lengthy questions and answers from the Larger Catechism. This may give you some idea of the importance of this great truth in the minds of those who wrote the confession and catechisms.

The first thing to catch our attention is the emphasis on the character of God, before the work of providence is detailed. The words "holy, wise, and powerful" refer not just to the action of God in providence, but more importantly, to the character of the great God who preserves and governs all His creatures and all their actions. In many ways, these are the most important words in the answer. Before trying to deal with the staggering reality of God's omnipotence as seen in providence, we must remember that He is indeed holy, wise, and powerful. This means that we may trust Him, even though we may not understand what and why in the working out of His providence, especially in our own lives. As believers, it is important to develop an attitude of trust so that when evil times come we may fall back on His truth and trust Him as our holy, wise, powerful, and loving Father.

A brief summary of this doctrine is in order. The Bible teaches us that God is sovereign in all things. We believe that our lives and the entire creation depend upon God for both origin and continuation. If it were not for the power of God, the universe would no doubt fly apart (literally) and we would no longer continue our own personal existence. All that is, is sustained by the power of God. His providence alone holds creation together and sustains or preserves life. In this overall picture, He also governs all His creatures and all their actions. Both the Old and the New Testament teach this explicitly and show this truth in action.

The great example in the Old Testament is the account of the exodus from Egypt. In every step of this inspired narrative, we see this doctrine working itself out in real-life situations. It begins with the preparation and call of Moses and continues through the actual exodus from Egypt and far beyond. Not only do we see God's providence at work preserving and governing all His creatures and all their actions, but we also see how His providence works. It includes events, circumstances, decisions, actions, and consequences. Special attention should be given to the fact that this includes obedience and disobedience, kindness and cruelty, the understandable and the inexplicable. At the same time, it should be carefully noted that the actors in this great drama are real people who are called on to make moral choices, and to act responsibly and responsively. Yet the one great truth that stands out above all others is that God is in control, not only of the final outcome, but of all the details.

In the New Testament, the story of God's providence centers on the Lord Jesus Christ. We see this in two ways. First He acts out this truth in His ministry. He provides food for the multitudes and healing for the leper. He calms the fierce storm and walks on the sea. He is not present when *the one whom He loves is ill*, but later calls him forth from the tomb. In all this and in many other parts of the story, we see him in the role of the One by whom all things were made and continue to exist.

In the next question, we shall deal with other aspects of this doctrine, including the more mysterious and painful aspects of providence.

Question #12: *What special act of providence did God exercise towards man, in the estate wherein he was created?*

Answer: *When God had created man, he entered into a covenant of life with him, upon condition of perfect obedience; forbidding him to eat of the tree of knowledge of good and evil, upon pain of death.*

The human race was created for the glory of God. It was also created for joy and perfect fellowship with the Creator. Adam and Eve were not only creatures, along with the other forms of life which God had created, but they were also children, in the image of the Father. They were His family. They were created in a state of innocence, nor were they guilty of any wrongdoing. Furthermore they were created with the ability to choose, which meant they could continue to perfectly obey the Father, and remain in a perpetual state of innocence with the implication of even greater things. When God required perfect obedience, He was not requiring the impossible. When man chose evil and disobedience, he was not choosing the inevitable. How all of this fits in with the doctrine of sovereignty is not explained in Scripture, nor should we attempt to explain the inexplicable. It is sufficient to note that Scripture affirms both the moral responsibility of man and the sovereignty of God. It is our duty therefore to also affirm both, even though we may not fully understand.

The Larger Catechism sheds a great deal of light upon this matter. In beautiful detail it describes the created estate of mankind and the favorable surroundings which were a part of the covenant God made with Adam and Eve. The Larger Catechism speaks of paradise, liberty, dominion, marriage, and communion with God. All of this points not only to the immediate situation of goodness surrounding our first parents, but also to the potential for future and perpetual blessing. This reaffirms the contention that it was really possible for our first parents to keep the covenant of works.

Obedience is never a matter of theory, but of practice. What could be more reasonable than for God to give to man a test of his obedience? The test was simple. Having surrounded Adam and Eve with all they needed, and far more, God required that they should not eat of the fruit of the tree of the knowledge of good and evil. We are not to think of this as some sort of "magic tree," but rather as a simple test of obedience. This is where the knowledge of good and evil comes in. Obedience would bring good. There is every reason to believe that if they passed this test, they would have been confirmed in their state of innocence forever. Disobedience would bring evil; in this case evil so great as to surpass the imagination of man. This evil would mean the loss of paradise and liberty, dominion, and communion. It would mean the corruption of marriage, and the end of that perfect fellowship with the Father which had been enjoyed from the moment of their creation. Oh, how much there was to gain; how much there was to lose.

To a degree the same is still true. What blessing is ours if we trust and obey. What misery is ours if we fail in faith and obedience. Death was the final consequence of disobedience, and it still is. We may rightly mourn the loss of innocence which befell our first parents by their sin. We may try to understand what a world we would have if they had only obeyed. It is far more profitable, however, to be amazed by the grace of our God, who in love predestined all his sons and daughters to be redeemed from the curse of the fall, and, in spite of their and Adam's sin, to some day be restored to the image and estate from which our first parents fell. All the precious elect will be restored and redeemed through the Lord Jesus Christ, and His great work of grace.

Question #13: *Did our first parents continue in the estate wherein they were created?*

Answer: *Our first parents, being left to the freedom of their own will, fell from the estate wherein they were created, by sinning against God.*

These words introduce us to a dark subject. This is the first tragedy in the tragic history of man. This is how Dr. J.B. Green began his comments on this question in his book, *A Harmony of the Westminster Standards*. He might well have added that this tragedy was the fountainhead of all subsequent tragedies, for truly it is so.

One of the basic flaws in modern anthropology and sociology is the failure to accept this fundamental truth about ourselves – we are a fallen race. Any realistic study of the human race must face the truth that we are flawed. The evolutionist sees this as evidence that man is evolving into a more perfect species, and one day will be free of all defect. Grace and redemption have no place in this erroneous philosophy.

The catechism is faithful to Scripture. It recognizes the truth of man's created estate. He was created sinless and righteous, in God's own image. He had a free moral will. He was not made to be either a puppet or a dumb beast, bound by created instincts to obey certain impulses. Nor was he created as a computer, to be programmed to automatically respond to certain commands. Commands were given in the covenant of works, but choices had to be made.

Neither Scripture nor the catechism explains why God created man this way. Both affirm that He did so. We may venture some tentative thoughts on why God made us as He did. If He created us for joy and fellowship with Himself, there must be a willing, knowledgeable response to the Creator on the part of man. Love and fellowship are only possible where choice is involved. If you married your spouse because you had no choice, are true love and heart-to-heart fellowship possible? In some Old Testament examples it does appear that, by the grace of God, mutual love and choice followed rather than preceded marriage. But if you marry her (or him) because you mutually choose each other from all other people on earth, then the ground is laid for true love and lasting fellowship. There must be mutual choice at some point if there is to be mutual love. This is the most logical explanation why God gave man a free will, and a necessary choice.

The catechism uses the expression, "being left to the freedom of their own will." This does not imply desertion on God's part. It teaches there was no coercion. Obedience must be a choice. Even in our fallen nature this is still true to a degree. In the state of grace, it is even more true. We are made alive in Christ. Our bodies are temples of the Holy Spirit. True, we still have our fallen natures in this life, but we also have new natures which enable us to make moral choices – not as totally free moral agents, but as redeemed and responsible children of the Father.

By sinning against God, Adam and Eve lost Eden and far more. The fall includes the loss of innocence, corruption of the will, loss of freedom, and above all (and most tragic of all) loss of fellowship with God. The consequences of this fall are too catastrophic to even imagine. Death and hell are involved. Pain, disease, violence, crime, cruelty, and oppression are also of the bitter fruit. Moreover, when our first parents fell, the rest of creation shared their awful fate. A curse fell on God's good earth that will not be lifted until the world is renewed by the finished work of Christ at His glorious return.

One final thought is in order. There is a very real sense in which each and every sin has this same effect. Someone has called sin "cosmic treason," and so it is. Never forget that your sin and my sin are just as odious in God's sight as the first sin. Flee from temptation. Pray with great seriousness of purpose, *Lead us not into temptation, but deliver us from evil.*

Question #14: *What is sin?*

Answer: *Sin is any want of conformity unto, or transgression of, the law of God.*

The *Westminster Shorter Catechism* is one of the truly great theological documents ever written. Though short and concise, it is thorough, clear, and always right to the point. It is remarkable that such a brief document could contain the wealth of material, the depth of insight, and the breadth of Biblical truth which the catechism contains. This question and answer are perhaps the best illustration of this. Here we have a statement concerning the nature of sin upon which we may expand, but it is very doubtful if any other statement could properly replace it.

Ordinarily we tend to begin any discussion of sin at the point of lawbreaking, rather than failure. If we include the aspect of omission, it is usually as an afterthought. The catechism begins with the treatment of sin where the Bible itself begins. Sin is basically failure. In fact, the word *sin* has its roots in a word that means failure. It is taken from the ancient art of archery. It means shooting towards a mark and missing, or falling short. The Apostle Paul said, *For all have sinned, and come short of the glory of God* (Romans 3:23). While it is true that Adam disobeyed God, still the beginning point was failure to believe His word.

Sin is more than just failure to act or to do. It is even more a failure to be what God wants us to be. It is failure to be as those created in His image. It is failure to be the persons we should be, who have been redeemed. This works itself out into many forms of passive disobedience, which, I am convinced, is more hateful to God than active transgressions. For instance, we do not trust as we should, which leads to the transgression of worry. Because we fail to love our neighbors as ourselves, we steal and bear false witness and covet.

So sin begins with failure to be what God calls us to be, which leads to failure to do what He commands us to do. Far too often we shrug off our failures with, "No one is perfect," as if this makes it acceptable. Of course no one is perfect, and that is serious indeed. Our Lord summed up His treatment of the law when He said, *Be ye therefore perfect, even as your Father which is in heaven is perfect* (Matthew 5:48). That's really the whole point. Anything less makes us sinners in His sight.

However, we cannot ignore the other side of the definition and still do justice to the Biblical teaching on sin. The catechism refers to transgression of the law. Another Biblical word is trespass, and these two words mean basically the same thing. Transgression implies willful disobedience, the intentional breaking of God's law. The Old Testament points out that even sins of ignorance, or unintentional breaking of God's law, are serious. How much more when we deliberately defy Him and offend Him! The sin of Peter, who was suddenly overtaken by unexpected weakness and temptation as he warmed himself at the fire of the enemy, was a serious offense, for which he had to repent and seek forgiveness. But how infinitely more hideous was the sin of Judas, who planned and plotted to betray the Lord.

Finally, let me suggest that there is another aspect to sin that is not really brought out in this definition, but which needs our attention. As believers, we know that God has become our loving Father through the grace of our Lord Jesus Christ. It is well to remember that when we break our Father's commands, we also break His heart. This alone should drive us to our knees, and even more to our Savior. As dear and loving children it should also break our hearts and motivate us toward a more earnest endeavor to be and to do what God commands.

Question #15: *What was the sin whereby our first parents fell from the estate wherein they were created?*

Answer: *The sin whereby our first parents fell from the estate wherein they were created, was their eating the forbidden fruit.*

Sin is never in the abstract. It is more than a theological topic for discussion or debate. Sin is a reality in the story of the human race. It is the common denominator of all people, for all have sinned. The origin of sin is never really discussed philosophically in the Bible, but the story is told in simple, straightforward narrative. The narratives relating to the early days of human life on earth are not in the form of parables. They are not prehistory; they are history, and they are told as they actually happened. The catechism recognizes this important feature of Genesis by simply declaring what the Bible tells us, namely, that the first sin of our first parents was eating the forbidden fruit.

Why was this sinful, and what was the nature of that sin? Adam and Eve were created in God's image with freedom to obey God and to enjoy His immediate and blessed fellowship. In their created state, they were also free to disobey Him and go their own way. It was necessary, therefore, for their obedience to be tested at some definite concrete point of behavior. God had surrounded them with goodness and plenty. They were given all they needed, and all that was best for them, in the beautiful garden of Eden. However, in the midst of the garden God had placed a special tree. It was called the tree of knowledge of good and evil. Whether there was some special physical property involved in the fruit of the tree we are not told, but that is relatively unimportant. What was, and is, important was the test of obedience. God did not tell them why He had given them this test. He did warn them of the severe consequences of disobeying, saying, *In the day that thou eatest thereof thou shalt surely die* (Genesis 2:17b).

So the first test involved was faith. They were required to believe God's Word for no other reason than that is was His revealed will. When they later questioned in their own minds, by the prompting of Satan, the reasonableness of God's command, they were but one step away from fall into ruin and death. We, too, are all faced with this same basic requirement – to believe and obey God's Word, just because it is His Word. He may give to us special reasons for believing and obeying, but sooner or later we are required to believe Him simply because He is God. Humanly speaking, the cross by which we are saved makes no sense. It is not according to human wisdom, and it is regarded as foolishness by the wisdom of man. But it is God's way and God's power for salvation, and we must believe it as such or be lost.

Another aspect of the test for our first parents was love for God and respect for His authority over their lives. Disobedience to His commands always involves a lack of both love and respect, and is, therefore, always a personal affront to God. Of all our sins we must say as David said, *Against Thee, Thee only, have I sinned, and done this evil in Thy sight* (Psalm 41:4a). Further, in yielding to Satan's persuasion, they chose their own wills instead of God's will. Self-indulgence and self-gratification became a basic drive in fallen human nature. Any time we choose our own desires over God's revealed will, we are demonstrating this same basic failure and flirting with death and alienation from God.

The final step was simple, outright disobedience. The act was contemplated, the pros and cons debated, the consequences dismissed as improbable or of little importance, and then the fruit was eaten. God's goodness was discounted. His Word was ignored, and even His purpose and intent for His children was questioned in this first sin.

Who can read this story with dry eyes? Who can read this story and not be convicted of his own waywardness and folly. *If thou, Lord, shouldest mark iniquities, O Lord, who shall stand* (Psalm 130:3)?

Question #16: *Did all mankind fall in Adam's first transgression?*

Answer: *The covenant being made with Adam, not only for himself, but for his posterity, all mankind, descending from him by ordinary generation, sinned in him, and fell with him in his first transgression.*

Fallout! This in one of the most dreaded words in the English language, when used in the context of nuclear warfare. During the so-called cold war, one of the most intense debates going on in the scientific community was concerning the extent of the potential damage of fallout from atomic bombs. While there were wide differences of opinion on the subject, all agreed that fallout would have worldwide consequences, with the potential destruction of all life as we know it. Some leading Christian thinkers suggest that this is the means God may use to fulfill end-times prophecies about the fiery judgement.

The catechism tells us of an even more deadly form of fallout: the consequences of Adams' first sin. Since Adam acted not only as a responsible moral agent, but as the representative for all future generations, his sin and fall affected the whole human race. The catechism explains that the covenant made with Adam was both for himself and for his posterity. In the language of Reformed theology, he was the federal head of the human race. Of course, this is not accepted either by humanists or liberal theologians. This rejection of God's Word in no way changes the reality of the consequences of Adam's fall. In fact, it simply bears witness to their share in Adam's fall.

We must assume that the effects of Adam's fall affected his entire being, body and soul. There is every reason to believe that the body God created for Adam was a model of perfection, free from sickness, weakness, and capable of everlasting life. If so, then it follows that sin brought about dramatic changes with long-lasting effects genetically. In fact, there must have been devastating genetic changes which were passed on to future generations in the form of sickness, imperfections of body and mind, and the inevitability of death.

In addition, there were even more deadly spiritual consequences. Mankind became a race of sinners under judgment of the holy God. Fellowship with God was broken so totally that never again could human beings come before this holy God by their own efforts. Lost, too, was their innocence. We often use the term "innocence" in referring to people. We speak of innocent bystanders, or innocent children. As a matter of Biblical truth, there are no innocents among the human race. We are all sinners by choice, but also by nature. Even our precious babies, though not guilty of sinful acts, inherit our sinful nature, which in turn expresses itself in time, and very early at that. Several years ago, a young lady, who had just become a mother for the first time, angrily upbraided me for teaching that children are born with sinful natures. "You can't tell me that my baby is a sinner!" she shouted at me. Actually, I wasn't saying her baby had committed sin, but simply that all people are born with a fallen nature. Even that failed to register…for a while. Less than a year later, I was visiting at a most inopportune time. The young mother was all dressed to attend a church meeting but had made the mistake of trying to feed the baby after dressing. I was never sure just where she had intended the pablum to go, but it didn't get there. Instead it was all over the nice clothes, the hairdo, the kitchen table, as well as the cat and the dog. The baby was screaming, the mom was crying, and the preacher was wisely backing out the door, refraining from any discussion of "original sin." As I remember, she threatened me with worse than death if I so much as mentioned the subject. While the incident was not without humor, the reality of sin and its hellish consequences are truths sad beyond a flood of tears.

One faint ray of hope appears in this catechism answer. All of Adam's descendants by ordinary generation sinned in him and fell with him. But there was a descendant of Adam who came by extraordinary generation, being conceived by the Holy Spirit, and born of the virgin Mary. He and He alone escaped the taint of original sin and offers to us the way of escape. Of this and of Him the catechism will have more to say.

Question #17: *Into what estate did the fall bring mankind?*

Answer: *The fall brought mankind into an estate of sin and misery.*

When Adam and Eve disobeyed God and sinned, they fell. It was a dreadful fall. They fell from holiness and happiness into sin and misery. This is one of the most fundamental truths in the Bible. It is also taught in the history of the human race, and in the daily newspaper.

It seems impossible, but there are still people who believe that mankind is getting better and better and will one day solve all the problems besetting us. Nothing could be further from the truth. The evidence to the contrary is overwhelming.

The catechism tells us what the Bible teaches from cover to cover. The human race is a fallen race. When the catechism uses the word *estate*, it refers to our condition. Man was once the prince of creation, but by sin he became the pauper, utterly destitute before a holy God. He was once the hero of the story, but became the villain, and the victim as well. The effects of our sinful condition are seen everywhere. We read of terrorism, drug-related crime, sex scandals, corruption in high places, disgraceful conduct on the part of well-known religious leaders. All this testifies to the sinful condition of the human race.

But we need not go that far to see this dreadful reality. We need look no further than our own hearts. When we would do good, evil quickly manifests itself. The good which we would do, we do not; and the evil which we would not do, that we do. Paul spoke of this in Romans 7, but we face it constantly in our own experience. It is not just that we commit sinful deeds, or even that we think sinful thoughts. We are sinful! That is our condition, that is the estate into which the fall brought us.

Scripture says, *all have sinned and come short of the glory of God*. But sin brings with it misery. They are never separated. To be sinful is to be miserable. Look at Psalm 51. This was written after Nathan the prophet came before King David and denounced his sinful behavior with Bathsheba, and the murder of her husband Uriah. David thought his affair with Bathsheba would bring him pleasure, even joy. Yes, there are pleasures in sin for a season, but there is never joy, and the pleasures are fleeting at best. David's doleful lament is the inner experience of everyone who ignores God's law. *Against thee, thee only have I sinned, and done this evil in thy sight.*

Later in this same Psalm we hear David plead with God, *Restore unto me the joy of thy salvation.* He knew what we all discover eventually. Fellowship with God is the source of joy, not sinful indulgence. The misery of our condition is clearly seen all around in the form of broken homes, abused and neglected children, forsaken elderly, incurable diseases, endless strife even in churches, and much, much more with which we are sadly familiar.

The greatest misery of sin is seen in none of this, however. The real misery, the source of all misery, is loss of fellowship with God. We were created by and for Him. Our purpose in life is to glorify and enjoy God, and anything less brings misery. I can still remember the misery in my childish heart when disobedience would break my parents' hearts, and mine as well. I can remember childhood spats with pals, and the misery of those broken relationships. I can remember feeling sad when my little children misbehaved, and our fellowship was broken. All of these memories help me understand that the estate of misery into which mankind fell has far-reaching and long-lasting consequences that are experienced by all people everywhere.

May I also be so bold as to suggest that our Father in heaven is also grieved by our misery? This is the foundation of our hope. Soon we shall consider that part of the catechism which tells us of God's answer to our sin and misery. For now, it is enough to know He has the answer, and you, by His grace, may know that glorious answer.

Question #18: *Wherein consists the sinfulness of that estate whereinto man fell?*

Answer: *The sinfulness of that estate whereinto man fell, consists in the guilt of Adam's first sin, the want of original righteousness, and the corruption of his whole nature, which is commonly called original sin; together with all actual transgressions which proceed from it.*

We find the defendant guilty as charged. How many times has this verdict been heard in a court of law by a person charged with a serious crime? It must surely be a dreadful thing to hear. It is a dreadful thing to hear from the Judge of all the earth, and it is His declaration upon all people, *for all have sinned...* Guilt is a reality in every life.

Psychology may attempt to help people deal with guilt feelings. Often these are misguided efforts which never deal with guilt itself, only the feelings which guilt produces. Christianity deals with the real issue: we are all guilty sinners in God's sight.

The catechism speaks of guilt as the inescapable consequence of sin. When we break a moral law, we become morally guilty. An act results in a condition, and repeated acts of sin harden us more and more in our guilty condition. Someone once said, "Sow a deed and reap a habit. Sow a habit and reap a character. Sow a character and reap a destiny." Our condition is one of guilt before a holy God.

Sin's consequences are not only guilt, but also a lack of positive righteousness. Because of sin, we are no longer righteous, nor are we free to be righteous. Once we sin, we can never again be innocent in our own strength, or by our own effort. God requires not only righteousness, but perfect righteousness for fellowship with Him. Adam and Eve lost their original righteousness, and we have never possessed it because we inherited a sinful nature. This does not mean that we can never be forgiven; it simply means we must be forgiven if we are to ever have a right relationship with God.

Forgiveness is what the Gospel is all about. Daily forgiveness is an abiding necessity for believers in their walk with the Lord. In addressing Christians, 1 John 1:9 tells us: *If we confess our sins, He is faithful and just to forgive our sins, and to cleanse us from all unrighteousness.*

Guilt and a lack of righteousness point us to a further result of Adam's fall – the corruption of our whole nature, or original sin. This means that our whole being is affected by sin. Our minds, our hearts, our wills, and even our physical bodies suffer because of sin. This does not mean that all people are totally and equally wicked in all they do, but it does mean that the poison of sin has permeated our entire being. Thus we are disobedient, selfish, lustful, and controlled by our sinful nature. Even when we would do good, evil is present. When these natural inclinations are unchecked either by law or grace, they become more and more dominant, and we become more and more sinful.

As the words of the catechism begin to sink in and the Biblical truths taught by the catechism become clearer, the amazing grace of our Lord becomes more and more precious. The greatest mystery of all time and eternity is why God loves sinners who are guilty of breaking His law, lacking in righteousness, and corrupt in their total beings. An equally unfathomable mystery is why He loves us so much that the Lord Jesus gave Himself for us. Mystery? Yes! But to that glorious mystery I cling, and by grace, trust in that saving grace.

Question #19: *What is the misery of that estate whereinto man fell?*

Answer: *All mankind, by their fall, lost communion with God, are under his wrath and curse, and so made liable to all miseries in this life, to death itself, and to the pains of hell forever.*

Have you ever watched a cute young couple walk down the street hand in hand? Wasn't your mind filled with thoughts of tenderness and admiration, and maybe even a little wistfulness? Well, here we see another sort of couple going hand in hand, and it is a terrible sight filling us with dread and fear. Sin and misery always go together. They can never be separated. It may take a while for this to be seen and experienced, but there is no exception to this rule. It is a spiritual law that is totally inflexible. No matter what pleasures there may be in sin for a season, no matter how sweet the fruit may taste at the moment, the inevitable correlation is that sin brings misery. The catechism describes the nature and extent of that misery. Go back and read this answer again. Doesn't your own experience verify this, at least when it describes the miseries of sin in this life? Pray God the final misery will never be known in your experience.

The wages of sin is death... These words from Romans are a verification of God's warning to Adam and Eve, *In the day that you sin, you will surely die.* The misery of sin begins with separation from God. Oh, how miserable we feel when there is separation from a loved one, especially if that estrangement has been caused by our sinfulness. But how much more miserable are we when there is separation from God. Sin does that. We may not always feel it at the moment. In fact, our own desires and emotions may blind us to this awful reality, and even lead us to believe that our sin is not really sin at all, or that it is somehow not quite so bad as others may think. We may even be deceived into thinking that in spite of our unconfessed sin we are still in close fellowship with God. We may even go on saying our prayers, reading our Bibles, and attending church. But, beloved, please hear and believe the catechism, believe me, and above all believe the Word of God. Sin brings loss of communion with God. That is why we must eagerly seek Him and confess our sins to Him quickly, that our sweet communion with Him may be restored.

There is more, much more, and it doesn't get better. Sin not only destroys our fellowship with the Lord, it brings upon us His wrath and curse. These are hard words, but is the Scripture any less hard? It is not until we deal with the full reality of sin that we may understand the fullness of grace. The Bible tells us, *God is angry with the wicked every day.* The wrath of God is a dreadful reality, even though many try to deny this Biblical truth. Too often we hear some well-meaning, but ill-informed person say that the God of the Old Testament is a God of wrath, but the God of the New Testament is a God of love. There are no words in the New Testament which exceed some of the Psalms and other writings which describe the tender fatherly love of God. There are no words in the Old Testament which equal in terror the words of Jesus and the Apostles in describing the wrath of God. Do not be deceived, the God of the Bible is a Holy God. And because He is holy, He has terrible wrath against sin.

Therefore, we are made liable to all miseries in this life, and to death itself, and to the pains of hell forever. Dreadful words! Sobering words! True words. Correcting words. Yet blessed words, for they drive us away from confidence in our own goodness, and we flee into the gracious arms of God's forgiving grace through His Son, the Lord Jesus Christ. He has said, *Whosoever comes to me, I will in no wise cast out.*

Question #20: *Did God leave all mankind to perish in the estate of sin and misery?*

Answer: *God having, out of his mere good pleasure, from all eternity, elected some to everlasting life, did enter into a covenant of grace, to deliver them out of the estate of sin and misery, and to bring them into an estate of salvation, by a Redeemer.*

The late Egbert Watson Smith, former secretary for foreign missions in the old southern Presbyterian Church, wrote a book, *The Creed of the Presbyterians*. In this book he said that before God had ever found a place in this vast universe to hang this spinning globe called earth, He had already found a place in His great heart of love for the elect.

This is the same truth taught in this question of the catechism. In fact, it is one of the great central themes of Scripture. It is the foundation of all our hopes and the source of all joy. The theology of grace begins with the character of God.

All God's purposes are consistent with His nature and flow from His nature. The motivation for God's gracious covenant is His mere good pleasure. I think we tend to miss the meaning of these words. To speak of God's mere good pleasure is to say that there was nothing in the fallen creature deserving of redemption. Nor is there anything a fallen person can do to merit God's good will.

The reason for His grace lies within God Himself. It pleases Him to love us poor sinners. It is His goodness, and His goodness alone, that moves Him to save lost sinners.

Another point the catechism makes is that His grace is from everlasting to everlasting. From all eternity God has been the God of grace. He did not decide to have mercy on us after the fall. His electing grace is from all eternity. We are chosen in Christ from before the foundation of the world.

It is well to pause for a moment and remember that God's electing grace comes to us through our Lord Jesus Christ. There is a very real sense in which the covenant of grace is a covenant between God the Father and God the Son. Some theologians speak of this as the covenant of redemption, which is the foundation for the covenant of grace. Christ Himself speaks of this covenant in His great high priestly prayer, recorded in John 17, when He says to the Father: *Thine they were, and Thou gavest them to Me.*

Who are the objects of His gracious covenant? The elect. God's grace is sovereign. He will have mercy upon whom He will.

Do not be foolishly tempted to lay the charge of injustice or unfairness to God. He is infinite in His wisdom as well as He goodness. Everything He does, every word He speaks, every thought in His mind is right and righteous and perfect. God alone knows why He chooses some to everlasting life. God alone is capable of understanding why. Don't be troubled by the foolish objections to election, or even the sincere misunderstanding of it. Rejoice in your own experience.

Does not the true believer understand that salvation is a gift? Do we not testify that our seeking the Lord was a response to prior seeking? Do we not affirm, *we love Him because He first loved us*? The glorious end or purpose of the covenant of grace is described in these words: *to deliver them out of the estate of sin and misery, and to bring them into an estate of salvation.* The darkness and despair of our sin and misery is more than matched by the glory of our deliverance.

The ultimate end of this covenant is that the elect are predestined to be conformed to the image of Christ, that He might be the firstborn among many brethren. Salvation from the curse and misery of sin will be complete when sin, misery, and death will have been forever banished from the new creation, and the covenant completed.

Question #21: *Who is the Redeemer of God's elect?*

Answer: *The only Redeemer of God's elect is the Lord Jesus Christ, who, being the eternal Son of God, became man, and so was, and continueth to be, God and man, in two distinct natures, and one person, forever.*

This is truly one of the most amazing statements in the catechism. Amazing because of what it teaches about Christ, and amazing because of how much it teaches about Christ in a few well-chosen words. In the previous question we learned the good news that God did not leave all mankind to perish in sin and misery, but through a redeemer He purposed to save His elect. In this question the identity of the Redeemer is revealed.

The first truth that meets our eyes is found in the word *only*. This is a major point of truth and should not be passed over lightly, especially in our day of easygoing toleration of almost any idea that poses in the dress of Christianity or any other religion. There is one name and one name only that deserves the title of Redeemer, for He alone can save us and bring us to God. That name is Jesus, or more properly, the Lord Jesus Christ. It is always well to use that full expression when referring to our Lord, for it includes all that He is:

God, man, savior.

Our understanding of who Jesus Christ is must begin with His deity. He is God the Son, the second person of the Trinity. The first chapter of John's Gospel is the clearest statement of Christ's deity in all Scripture. He was one with the Father from all eternity. He joined with the Father and the Spirit in the creation of the world. Later He said of Himself, *I and the Father are one*. It was for this claim the leaders brought Him to trial and condemned Him to death. The heart and soul of Christianity lies at this point. Jesus is God. He is God the Son from all eternity. Before Abraham was, He is.

God the Son became man through the incarnation. How He became man is the subject of the next question, but for now we simply affirm with the catechism that He became man. Here is the great mystery of our faith. The Creator entered into creation. He in whose image man was created became man Himself. It was not that He appeared on earth as if He were a man. He actually became man. He was fully human in every way.

In doing this He did not cease to be God, not for one moment. The two natures were joined together in one person. This makes Him completely unique. Like others before Him, He was a prophet. Like others before Him, He was a great teacher of truth. Like others before Him, He was a great leader. But like none before or after Him, He and He alone was both God and man.

This union of the human and divine has been the subject of theological inquiry and debate ever since the days of the Apostles. It is beyond human comprehension, but not beyond faith. He proved himself fully human over and over again while He was on earth. He also proved Himself God at every turn. He wept by the tomb of His dear friend Lazarus as anyone might do. But then He called dead Lazarus from the tomb as none save God could do. He was moved with compassion at the plight of the hopeless leper as anyone might be, but He cleansed the leper as none save God could do.

There is one final word which much be said. He is still both God and man, in two distinct natures, yet one person. Right now the Lord Jesus Christ is in heaven at the Father's right hand in the flesh of the resurrection body. He is God the Son as He has always been, but He is also the Son of Man as He became in the incarnation. Because He is still human, He knows our feelings. He is our merciful and faithful High Priest, who was tempted in all points as we are tempted (yet without sin). When we get to heaven and see Him, we will see the same Lord Jesus Christ the disciples saw on the first Easter morning, and the sight will be glorious and blessed.

Question #22: *How did Christ, being the Son of God, become man?*

Answer: *Christ, the Son of God, became man, by taking to himself a true body and a reasonable soul, being conceived by the power of the Holy Ghost, in the womb of the Virgin Mary, and born of her, yet without sin.*

The Lord Jesus Christ was and is and ever will be God the Son, the second person of the Trinity. The Gospel of John begins by affirming this. *In the beginning was the Word, and the Word was with God, and the Word was God... And the Word became flesh...* The catechism's concern at this point is to answer the question: How did this happen? The answer lies very close to the heart of the Gospel message.

First, the catechism affirms that God the Son became a human being, a man. This is the incarnation. His body was a true human body in every sense of the word. Though He was sinless, yet His body reflected the fallen state of man, in that it was subject to weakness and pain, and even death. He did not therefore inherit in His incarnation the body of Adam before the fall, but of Adam after the fall. This was in order that He might become bone of our bone and flesh of our flesh. He hungered and thirsted even as we do. His was a true human body.

His assumption of human nature was complete, for His soul was a rational (reasonable) soul. He had the capacity to think, to reason, to remember the past, anticipate the future, and even to dread suffering. He had family and friends, joys and sorrows. He was tempted in every possible way a human being may be tempted, in body and soul. That was a great comfort to me as a teenager; it is still a great comfort to me many years later. Yes, our Lord became a true man in the incarnation.

However, He was a very special man. He had no earthly father. His mother was a virgin at the time of His conception. Biological nonsense? Not at all; at least not for the creationist, and not even for one who calls himself a theistic evolutionist. The conception of Christ was an act of creation. The same Spirit who moved upon the face of the waters in the primeval creation, moved upon the body of the virgin Mary with the same creative power, and she conceived. It has always amazed me that the same person who believes that in the beginning God created a single-cell form of life that later evolved into a man, will not believe that the same God could energize a single cell in the body of Mary to cause conception. Of course, we who are Biblical creationists have no problem with miraculous conception at all, and this is a position I heartily recommend to one and all.

Let me tell you something. The biblical truth of the virgin birth is a very important doctrine. It is very popular in some circles to deny and deride this great truth. It is popular in some other circles to affirm it, while saying it is not important to believe in the virgin birth so long as one believes in the deity of Christ. The Bible describes the manner of the Savior's birth in some detail. This alone tells us that God thinks it is important, therefore so should we. It is a gloriously simple and beautiful truth. We receive it with wonder and joy.

Yes, Jesus Christ, God the Son, became a man by means of the Spirit's power in the body of the virgin Mary. He became a true man in every way. But he was not a sinful man. He was a tempted man, but not a fallen man. He was without sin. That is so important for our salvation. When He offered Himself to God on our behalf, He was as a lamb without spot and without blemish. Born sinless, sinless He remained all His life. From His throne, He looks upon us poor sinners with compassionate grace, and He will perfect that which He has begun in our hearts.

Question #23: *What offices doth Christ execute as our Redeemer?*

Answer: *Christ, as our Redeemer, executeth the offices of a prophet, of a priest, and of a king, both in his estate of humiliation and exaltation.*

I will sing of my Redeemer and His wondrous love to me... So goes the song known and loved by many who delight in Christ as their precious Redeemer. Here in the catechism we learn that Christ is our Redeemer and how He accomplished His role as such. The office is really one, but the functions are three. Before exploring the meaning of the three offices, let us first consider the word, *Redeemer*.

In the Bible we find the word used in several places and with various shades of meaning, all of which help us to understand Christ's work as our Redeemer. In the book of Exodus, God is Israel's Redeemer. This redemption takes places as a result of the Lord God coming to Egypt, and with a mighty hand defeating the gods of Egypt and their puppet king, Pharaoh. This is redemption by conquest. Our Lord Jesus Christ entered this world in which His elect are held prisoner by sin, death, and Satan. He waged war upon our fierce foes. In the famous battles of Gethsemane, Calvary, and Empty tomb, He tore down the strongholds of Satan, defeated sin and death, and set the captives free.

In other places in Scripture, redemption is the result of a price paid. We see this in the case of Hosea buying back his erring wife, Gomer, and restoring her to himself and to her home. In Isaiah, we hear God saying that He has redeemed His chosen ones by paying the ransom price. In the New Testament, both Paul and Peter make reference to Christ redeeming His people by paying the price for their release. Paul reminds us, ...*for you are bought with a price*. Peter tells us we have been redeemed, not with silver or gold or precious gems, but with the precious blood of Christ. The purchase price for our salvation includes the whole story of the incarnation and all the suffering and humiliation our Lord endured for us, beginning with the manger bed in Bethlehem, and including His life, His death, His resurrection, and His ascension.

Another concept of redemption is seen when the priest offers up a sacrifice to cover the sin and cleanse the guilt of God's people. This also includes the idea of substitution. God claimed for Himself all the first born of Israel, but provided that an offering of substitution was to be made instead of the firstborn. We even see this much earlier than the giving of the law, when God provided a substitute for Isaac on Moriah.

The doctrine of the substitutionary atonement lies at the very heart of New Testament theology as well. Christ is the Lamb of God slain from before the foundation of the world to take the place of guilty sinners before a righteous and holy God. He is the lamb God promised through Abraham, who said to Isaac, *My son, God will provide himself a lamb for a burnt offering* (Genesis 22:8b).

Therefore, in every sense of the word, Christ is our Redeemer. He is our king who conquers sin and death. He is our Moses, our prophet, who proclaims and demonstrates the mighty acts of God which mean salvation for the elect. He also reveals the law of the Kingdom, saying, *this is my commandment, that ye love one another* (John 15:12a). He is our great High Priest, who had made the once and for all perfect sacrifice for our sins, and who appears in the very presence of God, making intercession for us. He himself is that sacrifice.

These offices he performs as our Redeemer, thus accomplishing our salvation and preparing us for heaven.

Question #24: *How doth Christ execute the office of a prophet?*

Answer: *Christ executeth the office of a prophet, in revealing to us, by his word and Spirit, the will of God for our salvation.*

When we think of a prophet, a mental picture forms in our minds. We probably think of long robes and beards, of fiery words and fierce looks, of thundering messages and impending doom. We may think of Elijah and his contest with the prophets of Baal on the slopes of Carmel. We may think of bold Nathan and his fearless words to King David. Perhaps we may imagine Jeremiah, undaunted by the wrath of kings and nobles, but weeping over the fallen city of Jerusalem. For some, the picture of Isaiah comes into focus as he met with God in the temple vision, marking his call to the office of prophet. Somehow we find it difficult to fit the Lord Jesus into this picture.

Whatever mental picture we may have of a prophet, the Biblical picture of a prophet (far more accurate than our mental images) fits the Lord Jesus well, and the catechism helps us to see why this is true. In fact, the Lord embodies in His ministry all the best in all the prophets of God. Isaiah saw the Lord in a vision. The Lord Jesus has seen the Father face to face and dwelt with Him from all eternity. Brave Jeremiah faced the opposition of the king. Bravest of the brave, our Lord Jesus Christ confessed His own deity to the High Priest, knowing this confession would result in his own death. Elijah, who denounced sin in high places, knew himself to be a sinner. The Lord Jesus preached boldly against sin and was Himself sinless. So the comparison and the contrast between the Lord and the lesser prophets might be made in every case.

Just how does the Lord Jesus fulfill the role of prophet? In several ways. First, unlike a priest or king, the prophet of old was not anointed by any man to that holy office. The prophet was called by God alone and established as such in the eyes of the people by signs and wonders which accompanied the message from God. These were testimonies that the man and the message were from God. So we see Moses bearing God's word both to the unbelieving Israelites and stubborn, pagan Pharaoh. God granted him great signs to demonstrate to both parties that his message was from the Lord. To the Israelites who believed, they became testimonials to life; and to Pharaoh, who rejected the message, they were symbols of death.

When Jesus began His public ministry, He was anointed to the office of priest by another priest, John. His anointing as a prophet came directly from God, and the Father said, *This is my beloved son, in whom I am well pleased.* From that point on Jesus began to declare the will of God for our salvation, His preaching being accompanied by signs and wonders. Another aspect of the office of prophet, as seen in the Old Testament, was the endowing of the prophet with the Spirit of God, so that his words had authority and power. When the Holy Spirit came upon Jesus, and He went forth proclaiming the kingdom, the hallmark of His preaching was authority and power. *The people marveled, saying, 'Never has any man spoken as he speaks,' for He spoke as one having authority and not as the scribes.*

During His earthly ministry, our Lord was God's prophet, declaring His Word and will. But the catechism speaks in the present tense. He is still fulfilling that office as He speaks to His people by His Word and Spirit. As faithful pastors proclaim the Word under the power of the Spirit, Christ Himself is declaring the will of God for our salvation to His Church. Even when the Bible is read by the hearth or bedside, Christ is fulfilling His office as prophet. The Bible speaks of Christ, but it also speaks for Christ.

One final word is in order. The people of old were accountable for their response to the prophet's message. The issue was often life or death. So today, and far more, are we accountable for our response to the real and true prophet, the Lord Jesus Christ.

Question #25: *How doth Christ execute the office of a priest?*

Answer: *Christ executeth the office of a priest, in his once offering up of himself a sacrifice to satisfy divine justice, and reconcile us to God, and in making continual intercession for us.*

It is one thing to come before God with an offering or sacrifice. It is quite another to come before God as the sacrifice. As our great High Priest, the Lord Jesus Christ has done both for us. He is the once and for all perfect and complete sacrifice that atones for sin and makes us fit for the presence of God, now and in heaven.

In the Old Testament, the office of priest was ordained by God and regulated by His command. God appointed Aaron, Moses' brother, as the first High Priest for Israel. His descendants were to maintain the office of priest in perpetuity until Christ came and fulfilled the office. God intended Israel to be a worshiping people and required that their worship be acceptable in His sight. The responsibility of the priest was to carefully follow God's directions for worship and to lead the people of God in that worship.

The first step in acceptable worship involved the recognition of two things: God's holiness and man's sin. Those two things are still required of those who would worship the Father. He is holy, and we are sinful. Something must be done about these two realities before we may worship God in spirit and in truth. God's answer for Israel was an answer of pure grace. Sacrifices were to be made to atone for sin, and to bring the worshipers into God's presence. Atonement for sin required death, "for the soul that sins shall surely die." But God in His grace accepted animal sacrifices as a substitute for the life of the sinner. Of course, the blood and life of dumb beasts could not remove sin, but God removed sin by His grace and required the priests to offer the sacrifices in recognition both of His holiness and His grace.

All Old Testament worship began with these rites of sacrifice, so the believers could know God and at the same time know themselves to be sinners in need of grace from the great God who had called them to Himself. This constant reminder of sin and grace gave both joy and solemnity to worship. The ceremonies of atonement and cleansing pointed to the realities of grace behind the symbols. Each act of the priest was to teach specific truth about God, His holiness, and His grace. I encourage you to read again and with great care the passages from Exodus and Leviticus which describe the priestly office and its primary function of offering acceptable sacrifices to God.

Jesus is our great high priest. He offered not symbolic substitutes for sinners, but the true and perfect sacrifice: Himself in our place. He was *the Lamb of God who takes away the sin of the world*. He was sinless, perfect in His being and in His life of obedience. Thus, when He went to the cross and offered Himself up to the Father, it was the one and only, once-and-for-all perfect sacrifice. His blood was the blood of the everlasting covenant that makes atonement for all the elect and fits us to live with Him forever.

The priest had another function. His was the ministry of continual intercession. He prayed for God's people, seeking blessing and forgiveness. Here again we see the Lord Jesus fulfilling that function as our intercessor. We are told that He ever lives to make intercession for us. He became one of us. He knows and understands our nature and our needs. His ministry of intercession assures the blessing of God in our lives. His ministry of intercession also assures us that our own prayers are heard and answered as we come to the Father.

When He had made the perfect sacrifice for us, He opened heaven and tore apart the veil of the temple. Therefore, we may come boldly to the throne of grace, *dressed in his righteousness alone, faultless to stand before the throne.*

Question #26: *How doth Christ execute the office of a king?*

Answer: *Christ executeth the office of a king, in subduing us to himself, in ruling and defending us, and in restraining and conquering all his and our enemies.*

The late Dr. J.B. Green, in his *Harmony of the Westminster Standards*, said, "Christ as prophet meets the problem of man's ignorance, supplying him with knowledge. As priest, He meets the problem of man's guilt, supplying him with righteousness. As king, He meets the problem of man's weakness and dependence, supplying him with power and protection." We come now in our study to the last of these, as we think of Christ executing the office of king.

Christ is King! Make no mistake about it. When questioned by Pilate about the charges against Him, that he made Himself out to be a king, Jesus affirmed two things about His kingship. First, He said of the charge, *To this end* [being a king] *I was born.* Secondly, He said of His kingship, *My kingdom is not of this world.* By both statements He was affirming in unequivocal language that He was indeed a king.

He was also affirming that the origin and nature of His kingdom were and are heavenly. This does not mean that His kingdom has nothing to do with this world. Indeed it does! When we see the glorious visions in the Book of Revelation, we see Christ enthroned, ruling over the new creation encompassing both heaven and earth. But even now His kingship is being exercised on earth among His people, and the catechism does a beautiful job telling us how.

We use the word *sovereign* often, and often carelessly. It is a word that speaks of kingship. As our king, Christ has subdued our rebellious hearts by sovereign grace. I love the hymn which says, *I sought the Lord, and afterward I knew, He moved my soul to seek him, seeking me. It was not I that found, O Savior true; no I was found of Thee.* Truly this is the story of all who have sought the Savior king. He has found us. He has broken our stubborn wills with love. We are His people who have been subdued by a king whose crown was one of thorns, whose hands were nail-pierced. In subduing us to Himself, our king terrified us with the law, which brought conviction of sin and fear of judgment to come. Then when He drew us to His blessed cross, He cast out our fear with love, *for perfect love casts out fear.*

Once our king has brought us into His kingdom, we are His to rule and to defend. By His Word and Spirit, He teaches us His will, instructs us in His commands, and orders our lives for His glory and our good. Our Savior is also our Lord. We cannot have Him as Savior only; He is our Lord as well. The Christian life may be thought of as the process of learning to live under the lordship of Christ.

The other part of this has to do with protection. Our enemies are His enemies. The world, the flesh, and the devil all war against the believer's soul. Christ is the Captain of our salvation. He defends us against this deadly trinity of foes. Sin, death, and hell are our enemies, but Christ has defeated these dread foes as well, and defends us from them. Oh, yes, there are still battles to be fought, and as His people we are called upon to resist our enemies, but not in our own strength. As Martin Luther sang, *Did we in our own strength confide, our striving would be losing; were not the right man on our side, the man of God's own choosing. Dost ask who that may be? Christ Jesus it is he, Lord Sabaoth His name, from age to age the same, and He must win the battle... His kingdom is forever.*

Rejoice, the Lord is King! He has won us, He rules and defends us, and has willed that we will reign with Him.

Question #27: *Wherein did Christ's humiliation consist?*

Answer: *Christ's humiliation consisted in his being born, and that in a low condition, made under the law, undergoing the miseries of this life, the wrath of God, and the cursed death on the cross, in being buried and continuing under the power of death for a time.*

The human mind is incapable of grasping the truths set forth in this question and answer of the catechism. It is impossible for mortal mind to understand what it cost our Lord Jesus Christ to enter this sin-cursed world and win our salvation. The word humiliation is a good beginning point in our effort to at least try to see something of this purchase price He paid for the beloved elect.

The plan was from all eternity. The submission to the Father's will was a part of His nature from all eternity. The fulfillment of the will and plan involved great cost, great loss, and terrible suffering.

The catechism properly begins with His birth, not His cross. When you consider the pre-incarnate state of our Lord, when you hear the Apostle John begin his Gospel with the words, *In the beginning was the Word, and the Word was with God, and the Word was God...all things were made by him, and without him, was not anything made that was made....*, then you begin to see that the Creator, entering His creation, by the process of human birth is in itself the very essence of humiliation. The lowly circumstances of His birth serve to emphasize the humiliation. No room in the inn, the manger stall, the adoration of the shepherds, the flight into Egypt – all underscore the point: His was a lowly birth.

When God met Moses at the burning bush, He identified Himself as "I AM," the Savior of Israel, the God of the covenant. Later, on Mt. Sinai, He revealed himself as the lawgiver. When our Lord Jesus was on earth, He claimed this same exalted identity for Himself saying, *Before Abraham was, I AM*. Furthermore, He claimed for Himself the role of lawgiver, saying, *A new commandment I give you...* Yet He was made under the law. He submitted to the law He had given and kept it perfectly in letter and spirit, in form and substance. He honored the law in His teaching and His living.

When Jesus came into this world, He did not exempt Himself from any of the trials and sufferings of humanity. He was subjected to the miseries of this life, just as we are. He was hungry, tired, misunderstood, rejected, disappointed, hurt by failure of friends; He cruelly suffered, He wept, He was tempted and tried in every way we are. He shared our common lot. Few of us living in today's world suffer the degree of want and privation to which He was subjected, but it was the common lot of the poor, and He endured it willingly. What great love! But there is more to tell; much more.

The catechism speaks of the wrath of God and the cursed death of the cross. It is more proper to reverse this order and speak first of the cross, and then the wrath of God. When the Lord went to the cross, He was in fellowship with the Father and prayed that He would forgive those who crucified Him. Later, when in the mystery of His suffering, His soul was made an offering for sin, the righteous wrath of God fell upon Him, and the fellowship was broken – as was His heart, for He cried, *My God, my God, why hast thou forsaken me?* That wrath and separation were so bitter, so devastating, that we whisper in awesome wonder and with tears, *He descended into hell.* The humiliation had reached its lowest depths. He was despised by man, publicly disgraced and shamed, tortured and killed, and forsaken by the Father. They laid Him in a borrowed tomb, and there He remained under death's dark sway for three days. These things constitute our Lord's humiliation, *but He was wounded for our transgression, He was bruised for our iniquities, and the chastisement of our peace was upon Him...and with His stripes, we are healed.*

Question #28: *Wherein consisteth Christ's exaltation?*

Answer: *Christ's exaltation consisted in his rising again from the dead on the third day, in ascending up into heaven, in sitting at the right hand of God the Father, and in coming to judge the world at the last day.*

The exaltation of Christ is one of the major themes of Scripture, and it is the joy of the believer. Just before He left His disciples to go to the cross, the Lord Jesus promised them that they would see Him again, and when they saw Him, they would have great joy that could never be taken away. Later when Jesus appeared to these same disciples just after the resurrection and showed them His hands and His side, they were glad and rejoiced greatly. True to His word, the Lord gave them a joy they never lost again. The resurrection and the victory it represented became the cornerstone of the triumphant joy which has been characteristic of Christians for almost two thousand years. The resurrection of our Lord Jesus from the dead is the most important event in the history of the world. It was a true, bodily resurrection of one who was dead and buried. It was the first giant step in the exaltation of our Lord.

The resurrection, however, was not an isolated event. It may only be understood as the first in a series of events that are inseparable, and which comprise the exaltation of our Lord. Forty days after His resurrection, the Lord Jesus ascended into heaven. The ascension is properly recognized in the Apostles' Creed as deserving a prominent place in basic Christian doctrine. It is a neglected fact and truth in most preaching. The neglect of the ascension is most likely due to the fact that it is seen as a continuation of the resurrection. While this is true, it also has its own significance. This is seen especially in the book of Hebrews, which never mentions the resurrection, but makes the ascension the main focal point of Christology. The ascension to the right hand of the Father meant vindication for Christ. *The head that once was crowned with thorns, is crowned with glory now. A royal diadem adorns the mighty victor's brow.* Like the resurrection, the ascension was bodily. The glorified body of Christ, still recognizable and bearing still the marks of His suffering, was lifted up to heaven, where Christ began both His reign and His intercession. It was the vision of the ascended Christ at the right hand of the Father that gave to Stephen the courage to face death, and the grace to forgive those who murdered him. Undoubtedly the reality of Stephen's vision led to an even greater vision seen by Saul of Tarsus on his way to Damascus.

Dr. J.B. Green's *Harmony of the Westminster Standards* statement on the ascension is worth quoting: "While the Scripture and the Catechisms represent Christ as sitting, they do not represent Him as idle. Sitting is the symbol of rest, rest from work finished. But atonement accomplished, must be applied. Christ must reign, administering the affairs of His church and kingdom till the restitution of all things."

The final stage in Christ's exaltation has not yet taken place, and will not until the end of the age. He will come again to judge the living ad the dead, and until that day, His exaltation must wait its final glory. This is the blessed hope of believers, and the fear and dread of unbelief. Rightly so, for it is a fearful thing to fall into the hands of the living God. Our Lord Jesus will return in power and great glory, even as He affirmed to the High Priest when He was on trial before the Sanhedrin. To omit this truth is to ignore large portions of Scripture, both Old and New Testaments. Much of what our Lord taught during His final days on earth has to do with this great truth.

The humiliation of the Lord Jesus Christ is forever ended. His exaltation begun at the empty tomb has yet to see its final glory, a glory beyond all human mind or thought.

Question #29: *How are we made partakers of the redemption purchased by Christ?*

Answer: *We are made partakers of the redemption purchased by Christ, by the effectual application of it to us by his Holy Spirit.*

Presbyterians have always believed that Christ did not come to make the salvation to all peoples possible, but to make the salvation of God's elect certain. If salvation is merely possible for any or all, then it is equally possible that none will be saved. In short, condemnation would be a possibility for all. We believe that Christ's saving work assures the salvation of all those for whom He died. How could we believe less, and still hold to the sovereignty of God?

However, this certainty is not based on confidence in human ability to appropriate the grace of God, but in the power of God the Holy Spirit to apply the finished work of Christ to the elect. Again, we should understand that the elect are saved not because they are elect in themselves, but because Christ Jesus won their salvation by His perfect obedience in life, and His atoning death on the cross, and His blessed resurrection from the dead. The saving work of Christ resulted in God pardoning our sins and declaring us to be righteous in His sight and imputing to us the righteousness of Christ. We call this justification, the subject of a later study. But salvation is always an experience of grace and of Christ in the heart and life of the believer. This is the work of the Holy Spirit. He applies to us the benefits of Christ's work. By His work we are made partakers of what Christ has accomplished.

This truth is taught in a beautiful and comforting way in John 14. Jesus told His disciples that He was going away, but that He would send another Comforter to them. The Comforter would be the Holy Spirit, sent both from the Father and the Son to abide with His people forever. A part of His ministry would be to take the things of Christ and make them known to the disciples. This is not only a promise of illumination of the mind, but the application of saving truth to the heart. When Jesus promised that the Spirit would abide with us forever, He implied that He would be continually applying the benefits of His (Christ's) saving work to us. This would also assure our union with Christ, for the Lord promised that by the Spirit, He too would come to His disciples and be with them and in them. In fact, He went on to say that the Father would also come and abide with them. The Trinity is always present when one member is present.

Certainly, fellowship with God is a part of the application of the benefits of Christ's redemption. This alone wins for us access to God and fellowship with Him. To be partakers of the benefits of Christ's redemption is to be heirs of God and joint heirs with Christ. What glory! What joy!

I love the word effectual. It speaks of assurance and a hope that will not fail. It means that in Christ we will persevere unto the end. It means that we will be more than conquerors through Him who loves us. It means that even now we are the children of God, and that one day we will be like Him (Christ) for we shall see Him as He is.

Since it is the Holy Spirit who is at work to effectually apply the benefits of Christ's redemption to us, we must take heed to neither quench nor grieve the Spirit, whereby we are sealed unto the day of our full redemption. Rather it is ours to seek the constant filling of the Holy Spirit, and to obey Him as He opens God's Word to our minds and hearts.

Question #30: *How doth the Spirit apply to us the redemption purchased by Christ?*

Answer: *The Spirit applieth to us the redemption purchased by Christ, by working faith in us, and thereby uniting us to Christ in our effectual calling.*

There is logical progression in the catechism which is evident at every point. The last question dealt with how we are made partakers of Christ's redemption, namely by the Holy Spirit. In this question and answer, we see how the Spirit makes us partakers of redemption.

The Holy Spirit regenerates our hearts and enables us to have faith in Christ. More properly stated, the Spirit works faith in us. This speaks of sovereignty in salvation. This is entirely consistent with the Calvinistic theology of the catechism, which ascribes our salvation not to us for anything we are or do, but wholly to God. Another way of saying almost the same thing is found in Ephesians 2:8-9: *For by grace are ye saved through faith, and that not of yourselves, it is a gift of God, not of works, lest any man should boast.* Salvation is of the Lord. The Father elected us, the Son died for us, and the Spirit applies these things to us, so that we actually experience the grace of God.

We may not be consciously aware of the Holy Spirit's role in our salvation. The faith He works in our hearts comes by hearing the Word of God. This may come to us by merely reading the Bible or remembering something we have read in the Bible. It may come to us by direct testimony of a loving friend who shares Christ with us from the Word. It may come as a faithful minister preaches a powerful Gospel sermon that stirs our hearts, even as hearts were stirred at Pentecost by Peter's great message. The point is that we are apt to be more aware of the means the Spirit uses to work faith in us than we are of the Spirit Himself. We may even be tempted to feel that faith is something we generated in our own hearts. Often the Gospel preacher in his zeal will lay the burden of faith on the sinner who is dead in trespasses and sin. However, we need to always remember that faith is a gift of the Spirit – a gift to be received, and a gift to use, but a gift, nonetheless.

And what is the result of this faith? It unites us to Christ! What an amazing thing to consider. How rich is our salvation. United to Christ! This needs some amplification and explanation. We are united to Christ in His death on the cross. By this we have died to sin, and the benefits of His death become ours. We are united to Christ in His resurrection. This means our justification and the promise of our own resurrection in God's good time. This also means *Christ in you, the hope of glory*. Furthermore, it means we are heirs of God and joint heirs with Christ.

There is another side to this we often overlook in our joy over the blessings of this union. I speak of the awesome responsibility and high privileges inherent in this union. In speaking to His disciples, Christ said, *The works that I do, shall ye do also, and greater works than these, because I go to my Father.* By these words we understand that our union with Christ involves us in His work and mission. This, too, is a result of the Holy Spirit applying to us the redemption purchased by Christ. After His resurrection, the Lord Jesus gathered His disciples around Him and said to them, *Receive ye the Holy Spirit. As the Father hath sent me, so send I you.* Being united to Christ by the work of the Holy Spirit, we are made partakers of His redemption, and at the same time we become ambassadors of God and agents of the Holy Spirit, as He applies the benefits of Christ's redemption to all the elect.

Question #31: *What is effectual calling?*

Answer: *Effectual calling is the work of God's Spirit, whereby, convincing us of our sin and misery, enlightening our minds in the knowledge of Christ, and renewing our wills, he doth persuade and enable us to embrace Jesus Christ freely offered to us in the gospel.*

Sometimes the terms we use to describe the grace of God fail to convey the wonder and joy of our salvation. The expression *effectual calling* is warm and full, but it does not and cannot really tell the full story. First of all, this is the work of the Holy Spirit, the One promised by Jesus in the upper room to be our comforter. Because of His great love and wisdom, He will not allow us to be content with false peace, nor fleshly security. It is His will for us to know real peace and true comfort.

Therefore, the first work of the Holy Spirit in our effectual calling is to convince us of our sin and misery. This almost sounds like a contradiction in terms. The comforter makes us miserable? Indeed He does. For He is the true comforter. He must first bring us to the point of knowing ourselves to be *sinners in the sight of God, justly deserving His displeasure, and without hope save in His sovereign mercy.* He is like the skilled surgeon, who must inflict great pain if he is to bring about true healing. The malignancy of sin is deep-seated and life-threatening. We must see ourselves as condemned sinners before a holy God. The utter misery of knowing we are lost and without hope is a painful but very necessary experience, if we are to ever know the true comfort of forgiveness. This is precisely what Jesus meant when He said, *Blessed are the poor in spirit, for theirs is the kingdom of heaven.* Again He said, *Blessed are they that mourn, for they will be comforted.*

Thankfully, this is not the whole story. If it were, we would spend eternity in utter misery. However, a glorious next word, *enlightening our minds in the knowledge of Christ*, lifts the heavy weight off our hearts. Sin drives us to despair, the Holy Spirit leads us to Christ. As one Scottish preacher once said, "I looked into my own heart and saw sin and misery, darkness and despair, then I looked to Christ and saw light and hope. It is good that we met." When the Spirit enlightens our minds in the knowledge of Christ, He convinces me that Christ is the Son of God and Savior of sinners. He enables me to understand that the Son of Man came to seek and save that which was lost. He points me to the Word of God, in which I read, *All that the Father giveth me will come to me, and him that cometh to me, I will in no wise cast out.*

Once the mind is enlightened, then the will is quickened. We who were dead in our trespasses and sins are made alive in Christ by the Holy Spirit's work of regeneration. The desire for salvation is a gift. The will to respond to *whosoever will* comes from above. The old will with the powerful pull of the world, flesh, and devil is still there, but now a new will is given, and we are enabled to repent.

The work of effectual calling is never complete until, persuaded by the Word and inner work of the Holy Spirit, we embrace the Lord Jesus Christ, receiving and resting upon Him alone for salvation, as

He is offered in the Gospel. Drawn by cords of love, persuaded that I am a sinner and that Jesus died for me, I open my heart to Him who has loved me from all eternity, and by whose Holy Spirit I have been effectually called to Him.

Question #32: *What benefits do they that are effectually called partake of in this life?*

Answer: *They that are effectually called do in this life partake of justification, adoption, sanctification, and the several benefits which, in this life, do either accompany or flow from them.*

Years ago I read a story of a man who bought a ticket on a river boat going from Cincinnati, Ohio, to New Orleans, Louisiana. He had barely enough money for the ticket and was worried about hunger on the long trip, since he could not afford to eat in the ornate dining room on board the ship. Taking his last few dollars, he bought a supply of crackers and cheese – enough, he hoped, to last the long trip. Being embarrassed by his own poverty, he avoided the other passengers as much as possible, and during meals would slip away to his cabin and eat his meager fare. Toward the end of the voyage a fellow passenger who had noticed his absence during the meals asked him why he never came to the dinner. Much ashamed, he finally confessed that he could not afford the cost. Gently, his newfound friend asked him to take out his ticket and look on the reverse side. Upon doing so, he found to his chagrin these words: *All meals included.* He had made the trip, but he had missed out on some of the benefits of his ticket.

Those who are effectually called are blessed with many benefits which accompany and flow from this grace. Is it any wonder that those who have been effectually called by our great God have blessings and benefits from His hand? God is both great and good. He is a kind and gracious Father who delights to give his children good things. These good things are far more than just food and drink and shelter and clothing, as important as these things are. The benefits the catechism talks about have to do with the eternal and the enduring.

These benefits are summed up in three of the richest and sweetest words in the Christian's vocabulary. They are not words of theological abstraction, but of Christian experience and spiritual reality – justification, adoption, and sanctification.

What do these words mean, and how may we understand the doctrines taught by these words? It is often a temptation in this theologically illiterate day to simply abandon time-honored words which have been used throughout the history of the Church. The idea is that since no one understands the words anymore, we need to find new words to explain Biblical truths. The problem with this historically is that when we abandon Biblical words, we also abandon Biblical truths. This is how heresy creeps into the Church, and how cults begin.

It is also well to remember that these are not separate experiences or truths, rather these words describe the sum total of the one great reality of salvation by grace. They are facets on the diamond of the Father's gift of life to us in Christ Jesus. In later studies we will consider each one separately and see how each of these great words contributes to our understanding of the Gospel and our salvation.

Question #33: *What is justification?*

Answer: *Justification is an act of God's free grace, wherein he pardoneth all our sins, and accepteth us as righteous in his sight, only for the righteousness of Christ, imputed to us, and received by faith alone.*

Next to the doctrines which have to do with the persons and nature of the Godhead, the doctrine of justification is probably the most important doctrine of Scripture. It has always been at the heart of most controversies in the church since the days of the Apostles. In fact, many of the writings of Paul, especially the books of Romans and Galatians, center in this doctrine. The Biblical doctrine of justification by faith is closely associated with the doctrine of predestination, and logically flows out of it. Luther's emphasis on justification by faith alone and Calvin's teaching on predestination are simply two ways of looking at the same truth, namely that salvation is of the Lord.

When Luther rediscovered this great truth by his study of Scripture, the lid blew off the medieval Church! The prevailing view of justification in the church of that era was that man is justified either by good works or by the good will of the institutional Church, or both. There were those faithful souls who had been preaching salvation by grace through faith, but their numbers were few, and their voices stilled by the sword and stake. Luther's heralding of this historic doctrine became a historic event – a turning point in the history of Christianity. In God's providence, he lived to preach and write about this doctrine, and the truth spread like wildfire throughout Europe.

What is this powerful truth? Why is it so important? It is important because it deals with the most basic issue in life. How can sinful man be right with the holy God? How is it possible to have my sin forgiven and my guilt removed? Of course, if one does not take the Biblical doctrine of sin seriously, these may not seem to be overly important questions. But deep within the soul of every person, there is a dread and fear caused by sin, and the certainty of impending judgment. There is also a longing for God, and for the restoration of lost fellowship with Him – perhaps even a dim, shadowy memory of Eden when man walked with God in perfect harmony with the Creator, and the creation.

Justification means being right with God. It has to do with the forgiveness of sins, a right status and relationship with the Lord. The Bible makes it very clear that this is always based on God's sovereign grace. We are justified because God is God, and because He is good. It is His good pleasure to treat the elect just as if they had never sinned. In justification, God declares the unjust to be just. He pronounces the guilty to be not guilty in His holy sight. Incredible? Yes, but true.

How is it possible for a righteous God to deal with sinners as if they were His pure and righteous children? How can He love sinners, and forgive them, and still be the holy God? Does He simply ignore our sins? Of course not. He must be, and is, true to His own character.

Now we come to the heart of the Gospel. God sent His beloved Son into the world to live a life of obedience and sinless perfection. He fully pleased the Father in all things, keeping the law in letter and spirit. Then at the end of this perfect life, He who was without spot and blemish became our sin offering. He died on Calvary's cross as the Lamb of God who takes away the sin of the world.

Thus by His sinless life, He imputes to us the merits of His obedience, and by His death, His blood covers all our sins. We therefore are justified. God imputed to Christ all my sins, and He died for me. God imputes to me all Christ's righteousness, and I live because of Him and, by God's grace, for Him.

Questions #34: *What is adoption?*

Answer: *Adoption is an act of God's free grace, whereby we are received into the number, and have a right to all the privileges of the sons of God.*

Of all the human experiences in this world, the act of adoption may well come the nearest to illustrating the amazing love of God for sinners. This truth has received very little attention in theological studies, but it deserves much more. The Apostle Paul develops the concept of adoption more fully than the other writers of Scriptures, though he derives much of his theology of adoption from the Old Testament.

The catechism speaks of the nature of adoption and the rights of those adopted. First of all, notice that it is described as an act of God's free grace. In this it is similar to justification. Once God has adopted the elect, they are adopted once and for all. To be a child of God by grace today is to be a child of grace forever. Notice that the word *free* is used to modify grace. This simply means that the initiative is always from God. The comparison between God's act of adoption and the human act of adoption is seen most clearly at this point.

When human parents decide to adopt a child, they do not begin their search for someone who will love them, but for one whom they may love. The child to be adopted is usually unknown to the prospective parents. They are not obligated to adopt a particular baby, or any baby at all. They are motivated by love (ideally). So with God. Our adoption into His family is based on His free grace and sovereign love. We are made to be children of the Most High by His decree of adoption.

I love the way the Apostle John speaks to this great truth when he says, "Beloved now are we the sons of God, and it doth not yet appear what we shall be: but we know that when he appears, we shall be like him: *for we shall see him as he is.*" This reveals something of the privileges of being the sons of God. The first privilege is, of course, that even now we are the sons (and daughters) of God. The language of adoption is not only the language of love, it is also legal language. By adoption, we become heirs of God and joint heirs with Christ, the only-begotten Son. We are given the family name, and a new status as well as a new relationship with the Father. This means we have access into His presence and the privilege of prayer, with the expectation of being heard and answered. One thing many people do not seem to understand is that prayer is a privilege reserved for the Father's children. O yes, anyone may pray the sinner's prayer, "God be merciful to me, a sinner," but that is a prayer which will only be prayed, in sincerity, by those who have been regenerated by the Holy Spirit.

This brings me to another privilege of the sons of God, namely the indwelling Holy Spirit to be our comforter and helper. Finally, we have the assurance that even as earthly parents delight to give their children good things, and will not mock their needs, so much more will our heavenly Father give good things to His beloved adopted sons and daughters. And the last and best of these good things is a heavenly home. How glorious it is to be the adopted sons of God!

Question #35: *What is sanctification?*

Answer: *Sanctification is a work of God's free grace, whereby we are renewed in the whole man after the image of God, and are enabled more and more to die unto sin, and live unto righteousness.*

Here is a doctrine which needs much more attention by Presbyterians, and one which has been sadly neglected. If only the truth taught in this short statement of the catechism could be widely taught in our churches, there would be much less confusion abut this important doctrine. What is sanctification, and why is it so important to have a clear understanding of it?

To answer these questions, we need to notice three key words which appear in this answer. The first of these is the word *work*. Sanctification is not an act either of God or man. It is not instant, as some teach. You may not make some sort of spiritual decision which results in immediate sanctification. It is the work of God the Holy Spirit in the hearts and lives of all believers. It grows out of and naturally follows justification, but must always be distinguished from it. Like justification, it flows from God's free grace. Unlike justification, it is a work of grace and not an act of grace.

The work is twofold. It is a work that produces death. It is a work that leads to life. By God's work of sanctification, we are enabled to die more and more unto sin. Death is the only remedy for sin. It is the just punishment for sin. All people are born sinners, and thus born under the sentence of death, for *the soul that sinneth, it shall surely die.* Furthermore, it is by the propitiating death of Christ that our sins are atoned for, and we are delivered from death. In sanctification, what has happened *for* sinners begins to happen *in* sinners – the slow but sure process of dying to the habits and practices of sin. There is also a work of living in sanctification, for we are enabled to live more and more unto righteousness. The righteousness of Christ imputed to us is at the heart of justification. In sanctification God is at work to impart to us Christ's righteousness by the indwelling Holy Spirit.

Another key expression in understanding the catechism's doctrine of sanctification is: *in the whole man*. Sanctification affects the whole man. In this it is similar to total depravity, as Dr. J.B. Green points out in his commentary on the catechism. Both are total in extent, though not in degree. In sanctification our souls are drawn closer to Christ, our minds are renewed after His image, and even our bodies are touched in anticipation of the resurrection.

Finally, the expression, *the image of God*, shows us the true goal of sanctification. When God created man in His own image, it was never intended to be temporary. It is His purpose, from the very beginning, that the elect should be conformed to His image. Sanctification begins the process of renewal that will be complete in our glorification. The righteousness imputed to us, the righteousness being imparted to us, will finally issue in the completed work of God in our lives when we will be restored to His glorious image, and fully enter the inheritance of the sons of God.

Question #36: *What are the benefits which in this life do accompany or flow from justification, adoption, and sanctification?*

Answer: *The benefits which in this life do accompany or flow from justification, adoption, and sanctification, are: assurance of God's love, peace of conscience, joy in the Holy Ghost, increase of grace, and perseverance therein to the end.*

When I read the answer to this catechism question, I feel like a little child sitting under a Christmas tree opening up present after present of the most wonderful gifts. Or better still, I have the same exuberant joy that must have filled the heart of the Apostle John when he declared, *Behold what manner of love the Father hath bestowed upon us that we should be called the children of God!* Surely the Father has many gifts of love and grace for His children.

One of the deepest needs we all have is security and assurance in our relationships with others. How lost we feel when those whom we love and whose love we need make us feel uncertain and insecure. God never does this to His children. He gives to us assurance of His great love in so many ways. Above all He has given His Son. He constantly forgives our sins and draws us to Himself by His kindness and grace. His word is filled with tender assurances from cover to cover.

As a natural consequence of this assurance we also have peace of conscience. What a blessing and what a gift! The poet said, "Conscience makes cowards of us all." God's gift of peace gives us boldness to come into His presence. *Perfect love casts out fear. Therefore being justified by faith, we have peace with God through our Lord Jesus Christ.* Only those who have been oppressed by a guilty conscience can really appreciate this gift of peace. A friend of mine recently went through a long period of sickness and infection from an unknown source. Though his body was filled with antibiotics, still the infection persisted and even became life-threatening. Finally, the doctors discovered a small piece of metal in his lungs and removed it in a relatively simple procedure. Once it was gone, the infection quickly cleared up, and within a few days he was well again. When God removes the curse of sin and sentence of death by justification, He also gives us peace of conscience, and we are made whole.

Peace gives birth to joy, and this too belongs to the children of the Father. The Holy Spirit is the agent of our joy, just as He is the agent of our peace. By His ministry we are enabled to enjoy God. Christ promised His disciples that they would have joy when they saw Him again, and that joy could never be taken away. As the Spirit makes Christ known to us, and as He reveals the things of Christ to us, we share in that promised joy. This joy is in anticipation of the heavenly joy which we shall experience with the Lord. But even now this gift is ours.

The increase of grace simply means that the blessings and gifts from the Father do not diminish, but rather grow and increase as we walk with the Lord, in the light of His Word. The final benefit which flows from our justification, adoption, and sanctification is perseverance to the end. We persevere not in our own strength, but because God persevered for and in us. *He that hath begun a good work in you will perform it unto the day of Jesus Christ.*

Since from his bounty I receive such proofs of love divine,
Had I a thousand hearts to give, Lord, they should all be Thine.

Question #37: What benefits do believers receive from Christ at death?

Answer: *The souls of believers are at their death made perfect in holiness, and do immediately pass into glory; and their bodies, being still united to Christ, do rest in their graves till the resurrection.*

Several years ago, when I was a young pastor (make that a bunch of years ago), one of the duties which was the most difficult for me was the graveside service following a funeral. It was my custom to try to make the funeral service itself a service of worship, but the burial service always seemed anti-climactic at best. The worst part of it was the reading of the inevitable *dust to dust, ashes to ashes.* Then one day in preparation for a funeral service I remembered the words of this question from the catechism. What a contrast! Here we have a truly Biblical statement worthy to be read at the burial of a believer. I will always cherish the look of comfort of the face of the widow when I quietly quoted these words from the catechism. I have used this in every burial service since, and always to good effect.

However, one should not wait for a funeral before considering this great truth. The question of what awaits believers beyond this life should be of utmost interest to all Christians. Death is the common experience of all people. Unless the Christian faith can speak to this, and speak with great hope and assurance, whatever else it has to say would be of little consequence. Let us look more closely at these marvelous benefits which believers receive from Christ at death.

First, there is the completion within the spirit of that which began with regeneration. The souls of believers are at death made perfect in holiness. Sin will have been utterly defeated at that moment. It will no longer mar our character, nor hinder our closeness with the Lord. Because we will be made perfect in holiness, we will be in full and loving fellowship with our perfect and holy Father. Temptation will no longer dog our footsteps. The bitter pain of remorse will no longer disturb our hearts. This is the absolute necessity which must take place before we may enter our heavenly home. God will not permit sin to enter His new creation. In His infinite wisdom and sovereignty, He allowed the entrance of sin into Eden. The new Eden will experience no such invasion, for Satan will have been cast into the lake of fire.

There is no soul sleep known in Scripture. There is no purgatory which awaits believers. Our souls, being purged from sin by the blood of Christ, will at death enter into glory. By this the catechism is reflecting the theology of the Apostle Paul who said: *To be absent from the body is to be present with the Lord.* The entrance into glory is entrance into the presence of the Lord, ...*We shall see Him as He is.* Truly it will be a passage to glory to see the Savior face to face.

Finally, a word is included concerning the body. Our salvation is for the whole person. God has not abandoned the body He created for man. Though it has been horribly affected by the fall, it remains a very essential part of our being. The most important words in this statement concerning the body are these: *being still united to Christ.* How wonderful to know that the bodies of our precious dead are still united to Christ. How wonderful to know that God has a future for these bodies. Though now they *do rest in their graves*, there is a resurrection coming, and our bodies will then know the same glory.

Question #38: *What benefits do believers receive from Christ at the resurrection?*

Answer: *At the resurrection, believers, being raised up in glory, shall be openly acknowledged, and acquitted in the day of judgment, and made perfectly blessed in full enjoyment of God to all eternity.*

The resurrection of believers will be glorious beyond our fondest and wildest imagination. There will be such joy, such holy hilarity at that time, we shall be filled with praise and love for the Savior. There will be reunion with loved ones. Above all, there will be immediate and blessed communion with the Lord.

I read a story long ago that helps to illustrate something of that joy. A man and his young son were sailing on one of the Great Lakes when their small craft was caught in a sudden and fierce storm. In spite of the best efforts of the father, who was an experienced sailor, the small craft was overwhelmed, and the two were left clinging to the wreckage in mountainous seas. Within minutes, they were both swept away. The father's last glimpse of his son was the young lad disappearing beneath the waves. He awakened in a bunk in a Coast Guard vessel, realizing he had been rescued. His momentary joy was destroyed by the memory of his young son being washed away. As he turned his face to the wall to weep, he saw his son sleeping peacefully in the next bunk. He too had been rescued by the same ship. What joy was his in that moment of reunion! Yet it was but a pale shadow of our joy when we awaken on the resurrection morn.

The catechism does not dwell on the emotions of the resurrection, but on the immediate benefits which believers receive from Christ. The answer given by the Shorter Catechism at this point is something of a summary of several questions and answers from the Larger Catechism. Look these up and carefully study them to get the full picture. For our purposes, we shall consider only what the Shorter Catechism has to say.

First of all, we will be raised up in glory. This teaches the fact and form of the resurrection. We will experience a bodily resurrection and it will be glorious. Paul teaches us in I Corinthians 15 that our bodies will be raised incorruptible, powerful, and in glory. This will be a spiritual body, but a real body nonetheless. Having said these words, we still do not fully comprehend it all, nor do we need to. If we have trusted the Lord for our salvation, may we not also trust Him for the resurrection body?

Another wonderful benefit we shall receive from our Lord at the resurrection is acquittal, or the final vindication. Our justification will be affirmed anew, and we shall be acknowledged as being the Lord's own people. This does not mean there will be no accounting. Surely the Scripture teaches that we must all give an account as stewards on the day of judgment. For believers it will be a judgment of rewards, and vindication.

Finally, there is joy. We shall be made fully blessed. This means our relationship with the Lord will be completed. There will no longer be sin to mar and sin to confess and be forgiven. We will no longer walk by faith, but we shall see Him face to face, and our joy will be complete, and forever.

Question #39: *What is the duty which God requireth of man?*

Answer: *The duty which God requireth of man is, obedience to His revealed will.*

Duty! What a noble word. What a motivating word. For people in this generation, what a strange word. What an unwelcome word. For the most part, people are much more interested in learning about the benefits and blessings God has for us, rather than the duty He requires of us. But the two go together, and believers do have a duty they owe God. However, duty need not be a word to fear, nor even a burdensome word. Unfortunately, that is the connotation we have placed on this noble word.

In the Scriptures, duty grows out of a covenantal relationship between God and His people. The covenant is always predicated on the graciousness of God, and His initiative in establishing a relationship with His people. For instance, when He gave the law to Moses on Mount Sinai, He first reminded Israel that He was the God who had delivered them from bondage in Egypt. The gracious God of their salvation then gave them His ten words of instruction on how redeemed people are to live. The Ten Commandments are instructions from a loving heavenly Father to his children. By giving the law, God revealed much of His own character, and also the character He desires to see in His beloved children.

To see the law in this way does not lessen the duty we have toward it; indeed, it strengthens that duty. Love is always a stronger motivating force in the performance of duty than fear or even obligation. It is the duty of the parent to care for and to provide for the child, but the motivation is that of love, not mere obligation. Even though the young child may obey his parents primarily out of fear of punishment, later the main motivation will change to love, and a desire to please. So as we grow and mature in our relationship to the Lord, our obedience is an act of love, more than a fear of punishment.

Nevertheless, we do have a duty to our Father, and that duty is summarized in one word, *obedience*. Obedience, ideally, is like the love which motivates it, in that it is unconditional. We do not come before God and say, "We will obey your will if it suits us." Rather we come to Him saying, "All that the Lord has spoken, we will obey." Our duty is nothing less than this: to obey the entire will of God which He reveals to us. God has destined us to be conformed to the image of His Son, who is the express image of the Father. Obedience is our willing assent, and our eager anticipation of that glorious destiny.

The Lord Jesus said to His disciples, *If you love me, keep my commandments*. In these words we see again the motivation for doing our duty: Christ's love for us, and our love for Him. He spoke another word, which also motivates us towards obedience, when He said, *By this will all men know that ye are my disciples, if ye have love one for another*. Our duty is a duty of love. Our fulfillment of that duty is our most effective witness.

Question #40: *What did God at first reveal to man for the rule of his obedience?*

Answer: *The rule which God at first revealed to man for his obedience, was the moral law.*

The moral law did not begin with the giving of the ten words on Mount Sinai. When God created man in His own image He wrote on his heart the moral law. This is a part of what is meant when we hear God saying, *Let us make man in our own image.* Later, when the ten words were given to Moses, we discover that God was not only revealing His will, He was revealing His own character. Therefore, when man was created in the image of God, he was created with the moral law written into his very being. He was by created nature a law-abiding entity. Although he was given the freedom of choice in obedience to the Word of God, he was not neutral toward it. This is why his disobedience was such a tragedy. By rejecting the moral law, he was renouncing his own innate character, and his relationship with his God.

Nevertheless, the moral law was still the only acceptable standard of conduct for mankind, and he was held accountable for it, even though his sinful nature made perfect obedience to it impossible. You would understand that murder was wrong from the beginning, not just from the time when the Ten Commandments were delivered to Moses. We see this concept quite clearly in the account of the flood. In the days and years before the flood, mankind had become hopelessly corrupt. God looked upon the human race and said, *Every imagination of his heart is only evil continually.* The moral law was the standard that had been violated, and for which the judgment of God fell upon the earth.

So when the catechism talks of the moral law which God revealed, it takes into account His revelation prior to the giving of the commandments as recorded in the book of Exodus. There was in the account of the worldwide flood another way in which God revealed His moral law, which we may tend to miss when we read of this in Genesis. God revealed His moral law through His faithful servant Noah. It cannot be said that Noah perfectly obeyed and exemplified the moral law of God, but in contrast to the rest of humanity, the direction of his life was consciously guided by God's law. The Scriptures tell us that Noah was upright and blameless, and that he walked with God. All these expressions simply tell us that God found in Noah a man who lived his life honoring God's word. Furthermore, the New Testament refers to Noah as a preacher of righteousness. This means he both lived and taught the moral law. He obviously instructed his own family in God's law, for they were saved with him in the ark. After the flood, God's covenant with Noah revealed further details of the moral law, including the appropriate punishment for murder.

From Noah to Abraham, and down through the patriarchs to Moses, God was revealing His moral law and requiring obedience to it; blessing those who obeyed and cursing those who would not. As when He gave the formal ten words to Moses as the moral instructions for the covenant people, He was summarizing what was already known and given to mankind from the day of creation onward.

Question #41: *Where is the moral law summarily comprehended?*

Answer: *The moral law is summarily comprehended in the ten commandments.*

When God delivered the Ten Commandments to Moses, and through him these same laws to the nation of Israel, He was restating in summary all the guidelines for living He had revealed to mankind from the days of Adam and onward. What He required in the Ten Commandments He had always required. What He forbade in the Ten Commandments He had always forbidden. Let me remind you again of two basic truths which are essential to the understanding of this summary of the moral law. 1) The Ten Commandments reveal not only the will of God, but also His character. This implies that the commandments are intended to be not only guidelines for our conduct but also the mold for the shaping of our characters as God's image-bearers. 2) These commandments are not just a set of regulations but are primarily instructions from a loving Father to His children. The more we understand this, the more eager we are to learn them and live by them.

Although the Ten commandments are primarily intended for believers, they also form the foundation upon which civilization itself rests. No society of mankind can long endure without these basic principles of law and order. Even among people who have no knowledge of God and therefore no ability nor desire to love and honor Him, the commandments are still foundational to organized society. Certainly most of the civil law in the Western world rests upon this foundation.

A common cry from humanists and even unthinking Christians is, "You cannot legislate morality." Yet in every society there are laws against stealing and murder, with severe penalties for lawbreakers. This is clearly the legislation of morality. The ultimate reason why stealing, murder, adultery, and all other such crimes are wrong is because they violate the basic law of God. There is simply no escaping the fact that the moral law is summarily comprehended in the Ten Commandments.

For Christians, the ultimate authority for understanding and applying the Ten Commandments is none other than our King and Lawgiver, the Lord Jesus Christ. His Sermon on the Mount is the infallible interpretation of the Ten Commandments. In His sermon, He shows us the intention behind each of these ten words and what God requires in the hearts of those who accept His law as their standard of conduct. He never at any point puts His teaching in opposition to the law of God. What He does is to reject the traditional interpretation which had led Judaism so far astray from the original intention of the law. He takes it back to the original purpose and intent of the law. Therefore, it is the privilege and duty of all believers to know and understand the Ten Commandments from the perspective of the Sermon on the Mount.

As we shall see a bit later in our study of the catechism, the entire law of God is summed up in two great commandments: to love God with all of our hearts, and our neighbors as ourselves. In the final sense, the moral law is summarily comprehended in these two commandments, which are a summary of the ten.

Question #42: *What is the sum of the ten commandments?*

Answer: *The sum of the ten commandments is, to love the Lord our God, with all our heart, with all our soul, with all our strength, and with all our mind; and our neighbor as ourselves.*

Even as the moral law is summed up in the ten commandments, so the ten commandments are summed up by the law of love. This law has two directions: one toward God, and the other toward man. The Lord Jesus was so emphatic about this that He declared: *On these two commandments, hang all the law and the prophets.*

Since we have already seen that the law is a reflection of the character of God, it is clear that the basic element in God's character is love. This is why the Apostle John said, *God is love*. This does not negate the holiness or justice of God. In fact, these attributes are more clearly seen in light of His love. Because God is love, He judges and punishes the sin which threatens His children, and which destroys their relationship with Him. God emphatically underscores the relationship of holiness and love in the cross. There justice and mercy meet and kiss each other. The Father in love sends His beloved Son into the world to seek and save the lost. The faithful Son assumes the role of servant, takes upon Himself the sin of the elect, and endures the righteous wrath of the Father, whose holiness demands the punishment of sin.

When our Lord gave His summary of the law in Matthew 22, His words carried great weight, and they rang with sincerity because He had lived out His teaching in His life. Even when we are at our very best, there remains much inconsistency between what we say and what we do. Jesus practiced what He preached to perfection. Who could deny that His life was a demonstration of faithful love for His Father? Who could fail to see that He truly loved His neighbor as Himself? By His parable of the good Samaritan, He taught that one's neighbor is the one in need. He refused to restrict His definition of neighbor to the narrow confines Judaism had placed on the word. Furthermore, in His ministry, He lived out the teaching of His parable by ministering to the leper, to the Samaritan woman, and to many others who were outcasts and rejects. For Jesus, they were His neighbors, and He loved them with healing and saving power.

In the new covenant God has written His law upon our hearts. This means that love, as defined by the Lord Jesus, has become a part of our new nature. Believers are renewed image-bearers. We have a special duty and the high honor of reflecting the basic character of God. We are those who love the Lord our God with all our heart, mind, and strength. It is our greatest joy and chief end to glorify God. We demonstrate this by obedience. We remember that Jesus said, *If you love me, keep my commandments.* We also remember that He said, *A new commandment I give you, that you love one another, even as I have loved you.* The second table of the law shows us exactly how our love and righteousness go hand in hand. In fact, righteousness in our dealings both with God and man is the best way to demonstrate true love.

Question #43: *What is the preface to the ten commandments?*

Answer: *The preface to the ten commandments is in these words, "I am the Lord thy God, which have brought thee out of the land of Egypt, out of the house of bondage."*

Question #44: *What doth the preface to the ten commandments teach us?*

Answer: *The preface to the ten commandments teacheth us, that because God is the Lord, and our God, and Redeemer, therefore we are bound to keep all his commandments.*

There are only a few questions in the catechism which we will consider together, since they so obviously go together; and these two obviously must be considered together.

Why should the preface receive special attention before we begin to study the commandments? The answer is simply this: our attention to these commandments, and the degree to which we take them seriously, is in direct proportion to our knowledge of and reverence for the One who gave the law. Before God said, "Thou shalt" or "Thou shalt not," He first revealed Himself as the living and true God of the covenant, who has redeemed His people.

It is significant that this preface begins with the same words by which God answered Moses' question before the burning bush: *What is his name? What shall I say unto them?...Thus shalt thou say unto the children of Israel, I AM hath sent me unto you* (Exodus 3:13b, 14b). So now when God's chosen people are about to receive the law of the covenant, He repeats the same words again. As Dr. Green observed in his commentary on the Westminster Standards, "He calls Himself their God by a threefold right: by right of His nature; by right of His covenant relation to them, and by right of redemption." This affords a very good outline for us to follow in our consideration of the preface.

God reveals His nature through His name, JEHOVAH or YAHWEH. This implies that He is eternal and self-existent. He is the fountainhead of all life and being. He is the Creator and Sovereign of the entire universe. By His Word and will all things exist. It is He who sits upon the circle of the earth, and before whom all nations are as a drop in the bucket, or a speck of dust on the scales. By reason of His might, majesty, and power, His word is to be obeyed, His commands accepted as the law of life.

This great and dreadful God is the God of the covenant. He is Abraham's, Isaac's, and Jacob's God. Now to Israel, the covenant seed of the ancient patriarchs, He comes, saying, *I am the LORD thy God...*

There is an indication of the incarnation in these words. He is a personal God, who desires a personal relationship with those to whom He reveals Himself and with those whom He redeems. Such a relationship is only possible in the final sense because of the incarnation in which God becomes man in the person of our Lord Jesus Christ.

The sovereign Lord, the covenant-keeping God, is the Redeemer of His elect. *I am the Lord your God, which has brought you out of the land of Egypt, out of the house of bondage.* This mighty act of redemption was accomplished by means of the plagues culminating in the Passover. In this act of redemption Israel escaped the angel of death and the cruel bondage of Pharaoh. God also saved Israel from the more deadly bondage of idolatry. In His loving election, and out of His eternal love, He saved Israel and brought them into the land of promise. Gratitude becomes the motivation for obedience to all His commands.

We who are of the new covenant recognize His rights of Lordship, too, and for the same reasons. We hear the voice of our Savior God saying, *If you love me, keep my commandments.*

Question #45: *Which is the first commandment?*

Answer: *The first commandment is, "Thou shalt have no other gods before me."*

Question #46: *What is required in the first commandment?*

Answer: *The first commandment requireth us to know and acknowledge God to be the only true God, and our God, and to worship and glorify him accordingly.*

The first commandment is the first in every sense of the word. It is first in order, first in importance, and is the foundation upon which all other commandments rest. If this law is ignored, then it is impossible to give more than mere lip service to any other one. If, on the other hand, we take this law seriously, and sincerely try to obey it, then all others will fall in place, and we will delight in the law of our God. Think how much depends upon this commandment. Here is the foundation and fountainhead for godly living, for worship, for evangelism, and for all Christian virtues.

This word deals with the most basic and fundamental need of humanity...to know God. Secular psychology tells us that man's most basic needs are physical. This commandment teaches us the exact opposite: namely that the more basic need is spiritual. Our Lord Jesus reinforced this truth, when He refused Satan's temptation to turn to the stones into bread saying, *Man shall not live by bread alone, but by every word that proceedeth out of the mouth of God* (Matthew 4:4b). To know God and His will for your life is the deepest need you will ever experience, and offers the greatest reward and satisfaction.

In this commandment, God requires that He be given first place in your life. He requires that you worship Him alone as the one true and living God. This means much more than just formal acts of public worship, though His prophets of old said that His people worshiped him with their lips but that their hearts were far from Him. It is relatively easy to give mental assent to this law, and to obey it superficially, but sincere heart obedience to it requires our whole mind, heart, and strength.

When we build our lives around this commandment, as God requires of us, the priorities we establish reflect this. Sadly, our practice seldom lives up to our profession. We teach our children more by our actions and visible priorities than we ever do by our words of instruction, as important as these words may be. Oftentimes, a father may complain bitterly over Sunday dinner when the worship service lasts past noon, but thinks nothing of spending hours watching professional sports being acted out on the television screen. And have you ever heard a complaint when the ball game goes into overtime? If we tell our children that God must come first in our lives, but then spend so much of our income on material possessions that we have little if any left for the truly important things such as missionary work, will they believe that God is really first?

Obedience to the first commandment means that God is at the center of my solar system; all revolves around Him. It is this commandment which is really the foundation for the grand statement at the very beginning of our catechism: *Man's chief end is to glorify God and to enjoy Him forever.*

Question #47: *What is forbidden in the first commandment?*

Answer: *The first commandment forbiddeth the denying, or not worshiping and glorifying the true God, as God, and our God; and the giving the worship and glory to any other, which is due to Him alone.*

Atheism is a dreadful sin. It is a very common sin, and it is forbidden by the first commandment. Some might protest, saying, "You cannot command faith." That misses the point. The acknowledgement of God is more than a matter of faith. It is a fundamental truth, essential to the very essence of human nature.

We are beginning to see the impossibility of any human system built on atheism. The communist world is crumbling all around us. This collapse is basically moral and spiritual. The economic failure is merely a symptom. However, any political or economic system which is built on philosophical or even practical atheism is doomed to failure. It is increasingly and distressingly clear that our own nation, and indeed the entire Western world, is rapidly embracing atheism. Unless this is reversed quickly and thoroughly, Western civilization and all its systems and institutions will collapse, too. God will not be mocked!

It is a fearful thing to realize that our nation, by its law and courts, is more and more declaring itself to be one nation *out from under God.* Yet who can deny it? Christian citizens who have historically supported the public institutions of this country find themselves faced with more and more painful dilemmas. In fact, continued support of these institutions may force one into a position of denying God.

Philosophical atheism is a terrible sin, but there is another form of atheism which is also condemned and forbidden by the first commandment. I speak of subtle forms of atheism, such as confessing God outwardly, but then living as if God did not exist, or His existence were of little consequence. God Himself condemned this when He said of Israel, *This people honor me with their lips, but their hearts are far from me.* Insincere worship, though performed flawlessly in outward form, and though conforming to Scripture in a technical sense, is another form of atheism, as shocking as this may sound.

The Larger Catechism catalogs a long and dismaying list of sins forbidden by this law, and believers would do well to study question and answer 105 in the Larger Catechism in great detail. Let me suggest a profitable way in which this might be done. First go to your prayer closet alone. Get on your knees before God and read Psalm 51 as your prayer of general confession. Then with a broken and contrite heart, read the words of the catechism, slowly, thoughtfully. As you do this, examine your heart before God and ask Him to show you if you are guilty of any of these sins which break His holy law, the first commandment. You will, of course, discover that you are guilty of many, many of these sins. Confess them – each one. Pray for grace to overcome them. Seek His forgiveness for breaking His law and His heart. You will discover that, in so doing, this commandment will become alive and powerful in your life, and you will be motivated not only to avoid the sins forbidden by it, but even more to fulfill by sincere and diligent effort the requirements and the joys this law affords.

Question #48: *What are we especially taught by these words, "before me," in the first commandment?*

Answer: *These words, "before me," in the first commandment, teach us that God, who seeth all things, taketh notice of, and is much displeased with, the sin of having any other god.*

In the child's catechism, there is a question which asks, "Does God know all things?" The answer is, "Yes, nothing can be hidden from God." Our God sees and knows all things. Nothing is hidden from Him. We are all as open books before God. Therefore, everything we do, say, or even think, *is before Him*. Even the secrets of our own minds and hearts, which we ourselves do not fully understand, are known to Him. He is the God *with whom we have to do*.

The person who truly knows the Lord is the person who understands this and believes it. The person who fails to understand this may well be guilty of idolatry. Let me explain. If in all we do and are, we are conscious of the true and living God, our utmost devotion will be His. If we do not keep Him in our conscious awareness at all times, we will likely put other things in the throne room of our lives, and thus become idolaters. These idols may have many forms and many names, but unless God Himself comes first, another has taken His place of chief affection in our hearts. This is the very essence of idolatry.

It is so very important to understand that God not only sees all things, but takes notice of them, too. He takes special notice of our obedience or disobedience to this first commandment. He is much pleased when His children attend to all its duties. He is much displeased and grieved when we are guilty of the sins it forbids.

We see something of this in the book of Ezekiel. In the eighth chapter we read of a vision which God gave Ezekiel – a vision in which he was taken in the spirit to the temple of the Lord in Jerusalem. There Ezekiel saw Israel committing detestable idolatry. In hidden places, even the spiritual leaders were engaged in secret idolatry. But God saw, and God knew, and God was grieved and insulted by what He saw. He said to Ezekiel, *I will deal with them in anger; I will not look on them with pity or spare them. Although they shout in my ears, I will not hear them.* God is no less displeased by our idols of materialism, wealth, and luxury. Even though we may make lip profession of true worship, and even attend with regularity the house of God, there may well be hidden rooms where our affection, love, and desires are given over to our private idols. Please know that God sees this. Please understand He is insulted and grieved by it.

Even as I write these things, my heart is convicted. I trust your heart will be touched as you read and ponder. Join with me in the sincere prayer of the Psalmist of old, who cried out to God, *Search me, O God, and know my heart: try me and know my thoughts: and see if there be any wicked way in me, and lead me in the way everlasting.* Yes, *God knoweth the secrets of the heart.* If we are near the heart of God, we will be aware of our sin; and being aware of it, we will repent and have no other gods before Him.

Question #49: *Which is the second commandment?*

Answer: *The second commandment is, "Thou shalt not make unto thee any graven image, or any likeness of any thing that is in the heaven above, or that is in the earth beneath, or that is in the water under the earth: thou shalt not bow down to them, nor serve them: for I the Lord thy God am a jealous God, visiting the iniquity of the fathers upon the children unto the third and fourth generation of them that hate me; and shewing mercy unto thousands of them that love me, and keep my commandments."*

Idolatry, in one form or another, has been the bane of humanity from the dawn of history, and is still with us even to this day. The genesis of idolatry is in the mind of man, fallen man. God created man in His own image, and after the fall, man set out to attempt to create God in his image. This is idolatry.

Men of old sought out skilled craftsmen who fashioned idols from precious metal to give a visual representation to their mental and emotional images of what they wanted their god to be. Then they fell down and worshiped this god of their imagination. Though it was nothing more than cunningly designed metal, yet men ascribed to the idol great powers. They prayed to it as though its ears could actually hear. They sought guidance from it as though it had eyes that could see. They sought compassion from the cold statue with no heart. Poor men, who could not afford the golden gods, simply carved images from stumps, and worshiped with equal fervency, and equal futility.

Modern man, though more sophisticated, is no less idolatrous. He still worships gods of silver and gold, or now maybe gods of electronics and microchips. The gods of wealth, power, affluence, and sensuality have captured the minds and hearts of people today as no stone or metal image could ever do in ancient days. What thinking person could fail to see the tremendous hold these modern gods have on people today?

Many Christians ignore this prohibition and worship, or attempt to worship, God through images, statues, pictures, and man-made rituals and forms. They would claim that these things are merely aids to worship, but by so doing they refuse God's authority to command the method and nature of true worship.

It is also possible to elevate our own ideas of what we think God is like to the level of Biblical revelation, and even above it. I have been in Bible studies with people who insist that their ideas of what God is like are more important than the doctrine of God found in Scripture. Such presumption is most insulting to God, who has faithfully revealed Himself in His word. How often I have heard people reject the Biblical concepts of God's righteousness, His absolute sovereignty, or His terrible wrath against sin. When presented with these truths they will respond, "I could never believe in a God who would send people to hell" or "I don't think God would predestine some people to be saved." To reject any of the attributes of God in favor of a God acceptable to fallen human reason is a clear and dangerous violation of the second commandment.

The God who reveals Himself in Scripture is the one true God, and anything less or other is an idol, a graven image of a corrupt mind. To such images we must not fall down or offer worship.

Question #50: *What is required in the second commandment?*

Answer: *The second commandment requireth the receiving, observing, and keeping pure and entire, all such religious worship and ordinances as God hath appointed in his Word.*

Question #51: *What is forbidden in the second commandment?*

Answer: *The second commandment forbiddeth the worshiping of God by images, or any other way not appointed in his word.*

Worship is exceedingly important to God. He seeks those who will worship Him in spirit and in truth. The primary occupation of heaven is worship. The glorious climax of all human history is the gathering of the redeemed before the throne of God and of the Lamb, to offer grateful and joyous praise and worship. Is it any wonder that God should direct us in how He desires to be worshiped?

These two questions and answers from the catechism offer very explicit directions on how to worship God correctly and how to avoid offending Him by our worship. In this careless age of *every man doing what is right in his own eyes*, we would do well to give serious attention to this matter. There is a feeling abroad that everyone should have the right to worship God as he or she sees fit. This may be a right conferred by the laws of men, but it is not a right given by the law of our God. He requires that we worship Him as He sees fit, and as He directs in His word. Worship that is not according to God's word is worship that violates the second commandment.

The Larger Catechism gives details not covered by the Shorter and is an effective commentary on the Shorter Catechism. Under the heading of what is required, the Larger Catechism spells out such elements as prayer and thanksgiving in the name of Christ. This would include not only prayers, but also thanksgiving in song, by singing, as the Apostle Paul instructed, *psalms and hymns, and spiritual songs.*

This commandment also requires that the Word be read and expounded. I was recently in a worship service in which a beautiful passage from God's Word was read. However, the sermon which followed had little if anything to do with that passage or any other passage from the Bible. On the other hand, I have attended worship services (yes, even Presbyterian worship services) in which only one verse of Scripture was read in the entire service. In both cases there was an absence of very necessary elements of worship.

The Larger Catechism points out that the observance of the sacraments is a proper part of worship as well.

The Larger Catechism is also helpful in understanding those things forbidden by this commandment. Not only are we to avoid any forms of worship contrary to the Word, but also any images of God, either inwardly of the mind, or outwardly in any kind of image or likeness. We are also warned against accepting traditions of worship which do not come from the Word. This is a sword with two edges, for it not only speaks against liturgical practices of non-Reformed traditions, but many worship practices defended on the grounds of Reformed tradition as well, with no real Biblical case for that particular practice.

What it all comes down to is this: God desires and requires of us that we worship Him in spirit and in truth, and He reserves for Himself alone the right to define and describe that true worship. He has revealed these things in His word and expects His children to take this revelation seriously, even as they take worship seriously.

Question #52: *What are the reasons annexed to the second commandment?*

Answer: *The reasons annexed to the second commandment are: God's sovereignty over us, his propriety in us, and the zeal he hath to his own worship.*

When God gives a commandment to His people, it is to be regarded with respect, reverence, and eager obedience. When He gives specific reasons for the commandment, as He does with the second commandment, we are expected to give special notice and attention.

In the Lord's Prayer, there is one petition which deserves special notice because it is the only one which our Lord reinforces with specific promises and warnings. That petition is, *forgive us our debts, as we forgive our debtors.* He then added these words, *for if ye forgive men their trespasses, your heavenly Father will also forgive you: but if ye forgive not men their trespasses, neither will your Father forgive your trespasses* (Matthew 6:12, 14). These words place special emphasis on this petition of the Lord's Prayer.

So in the second commandment, we have additional words of special emphasis which focus our attention on the importance of obedience.

God gives us three reasons why idolatry is so odious to Him, and why proper worship is so important: (1) His Lordship over our lives; (2) His image in us; and (3) His own zeal for true worship. Any one of these reasons is compelling; all three together are overwhelming.

God is our sovereign Lord. He alone deserves our worship and praise. He brooks no rivals. He has every right to require our worship and to instruct us in proper worship. Idolatry is a denial of this right. It is a rejection of His sovereignty. It is questioning His authority and even His integrity. Eve's first step in sin was not eating the forbidden fruit, it was listening when Satan questioned God's good purpose in the prohibition of that fruit. Cain's offering was rejected because his heart was not right with God, but there may be some indication that neither was his worship right with God. In the parable of the wedding feast, Jesus told of the man who refused the wedding garment and was expelled from the feast, presumably because his refusal was a denial of the prerogative of the host to invite and clothe his guests as he saw fit. May we not draw some lesson from this concerning worship? How dare we insult the character of God by offering to Him worship which is displeasing to Him?

The second reason is stated this way: *His propriety in us.* This really speaks of the image of God in us which makes worship and the manner of worship so very important. Because we are image-bearers of the sovereign God, only God-directed worship is appropriate. Idolatry is a denial that we are image-bearers of the one true God. It would be most fitting for the evolutionists to worship a god made in the image of a monkey, or any other beast, since they insist that we all evolved from lower forms of life. There is a sense in which all idolaters are evolutionists, and vice versa.

Finally, our obedience to this commandment is important for us because it is important to God. If He is zealous for true worship, then so must we be. The Father seeks true worshipers, and in true worship we seek to honor the one true and living God.

Question #53: *Which is the third commandment?*

Answer: *The third commandment is, "Thou shalt not take the name of the Lord thy God in vain; for the Lord will not hold him guiltless that taketh his name in vain."*

High on the list of God's priorities is the sacredness of His name. One of the evidences of a society dominated by atheism is a disregard for this sanctity. Needless to say, we are living in just this kind of society. The name of God is held in ridicule rather than reverence. We are living in a society that is openly defying God, and almost daring Him to do something about it. The warning, *for God will not hold him guiltless that taketh his name in vain*, is ignored and mocked.

Have you ever considered why God's name is so important to Him, and to us? The reason is simple: it is far more than just a word; it represents and reveals who His is. Your name is important to you for the same reason. Each individual within a family bears the family name and must faithfully represent the integrity of that name. Far more important than any earthly name is the name of our Father in heaven. He holds it in high esteem and requires the same of us. Any irreverent or flippant use of His name is offensive to Him and invites His displeasure, and even His wrath. At the same time, the use of His name in a reverent and loving manner honors and pleases Him. The ancient Hebrews seldom spoke or even wrote the name by which God revealed Himself to Moses. This is one reason why we find the word LORD (note the capital letters) so often in Scripture rather than the name *Yahweh*, or *Jehovah*. They were fearful of using that holy name improperly, and so avoided its use in most cases. Some scholars tell us that only the High Priest spoke aloud this name of God, and that only on special occasions of great solemnity.

In contrast to this extreme (if indeed it was an extreme), the modern believer seems influenced by the profane culture in which we live, to the extent that we join the world in its sin of taking God's name in vain. It never ceases to distress me to hear Christians using God's name lightly, and even irreverently. It has become a common expression to say, "oh, God" or "good God" as a term of shock, dismay, or surprise. It is hard to say which is more destructive to the minds of the young: to be constantly exposed to the profane use of God's name on radio and television, or for Christian parents to fail in their duty to teach the sacredness of God's name and to hold it in loving esteem.

One of the great responsibilities which rests upon all believers is to live in such a way that God's name will be respected and honored because of our conduct. It was once said of King David that the heathen blasphemed the name of God because of his conduct. May this never be said of us! Rather, may people who see, hear, and know us bless the name of our God and, even more, call upon Him for salvation and life. Thus we honor Him and give heart obedience to this commandment.

Question #54: *What is required in the third commandment?*

Answer: *The third commandment requireth the holy and reverent use of God's names, titles, attributes, ordinances, word, and works.*

Question #55: *What is forbidden in the third commandment?*

Answer: *The third commandment forbiddeth all profaning or abusing of anything whereby God maketh himself known.*

The third commandment which God has given to His people carries with it the responsibility of the right use of His name, and the avoiding of the wrong use. Both aspects of obedience are equally important; therefore, we will consider both questions from the catechism together.

To understand the requirements for the proper use of God's name, we must deal with the words *holy* and *reverent*. We should take great delight and feel freedom in our use of God's name, so long as we keep in mind these two words. There is a hymn which sings, *How sweet the name of Jesus sounds in a believer's ear!* Truly the names by which our God has revealed Himself to us are sweet and glorious, and we love to repeat them over and over again. We do this in a spirit of reverent and holy joy, whether in the privacy of our own prayer closets or in public assemblies of worship. The holy and reverent use of God's names and titles requires a knowledge and an understanding of who God is and what He has done in His works of creation, providence, and redemption. As we read His word and gain this understanding, we are awed by His holiness and majesty, as well as His grace and mercy. Therefore, when we speak or even think His name, we do so with reverence and with love.

To use His name properly, we must use it often in prayer and praise. We must speak it often in witness and testimony. How often and in what spirit we use the name of our God is a good indication of our relationship with Him. I think back years ago when my firstborn was on the mission field as a young single lady. She met a fellow missionary who would one day be her husband. Her first reference to him in a letter was rather casual. Soon, however, his name was mentioned throughout every letter, and with growing and even glowing appreciation and affection. Her use of his name was a fair indication of the relationship which had blossomed into love. So the name of our Lord and our God becomes increasingly dear as we grow in our relationship with Him.

Needless to say, the improper or profane use of God's names or titles is forbidden by this holy law. In an age and society in which profanity and obscenity are commonplace, the believer is required to maintain a good testimony of pure, wholesome speech. Parents should not be overly surprised to hear profanity on the lips of their children if there is no parental supervision and even censorship of what their children watch on television or hear on the radio. It is almost impossible to watch a single program without hearing God's name taken in an irreverent manner. When this happens, either change the channel or turn it off, and tell your children why. Many children who attend public and private schools hear their teachers take God's name in vain constantly. They should be protected from this form of child abuse, even if it means changing schools or home schooling. Don't underestimate the devastating effect constant exposure to profanity will have on your children.

There is another more subtle sin which is seldom mentioned in connection with this commandment, yet lies at the very heart of its meaning. This is the sin of insincerity. When we use God's name in worship that does not come from the heart, we take His name in vain. When our basic profession of faith is insincere, we take His name in vain. When we offer prayers unworthy of our Savior's name, we take His name in vain.

Eternal vigilance is the price of freedom and this same kind of commitment is required of those who would obey this law of God.

Question #56: *What is the reason annexed to the third commandment?*

Answer: *The reason annexed to the third commandment is, that however the breakers of this commandment may escape punishment from men, yet the Lord our God will not suffer them to escape his righteous judgment.*

The seriousness of this commandment is underscored by the warning attached to it. It is the only commandment with such a warning. God takes the sacredness of His name very seriously indeed. The day has long ceased when there were laws against public profanity, though such laws were once on the books of almost every state and municipality in the United States. If such laws did not exist it was because they were not needed, since there was a public consensus that profanity was improper. God's laws are still "on the books" and in the Book.

Does this mean that the breaking of this commandment is the unforgivable sin? No, there is nothing in Scripture to suggest this. However, it is most certainly a heinous sin in God's sight and hearing. It is interesting to note that Jesus warned that blasphemy against the Holy Spirit would not be forgiven. Although theologians and other biblical scholars disagree as to the exact nature of the *sin against the Holy Spirit*, certainly the sin of taking God's name in vain is closely akin to blasphemy. The point is that God gives a special waring against this sin, and this warning should be taken seriously.

There are other consequences resulting from disobedience to this commandment. The loss of fellowship with the Lord is one of the more serious. When we carelessly or deliberately abuse the name of some earthly friend and fail to show respect and regard for their good name, our relationship is diminished and even seriously threatened. How much more will our disrespectful use of God's name hinder our fellowship with Him?

The fear of the Lord is the beginning of wisdom. Lack of reverence for Him and His holy name is the foundation of all folly.

If we do not hold His name in reverence, if we do not honor and respect Him, are we likely to honor and respect those made in His image? Have you ever noticed how those who never seem to have anything but contempt for their fellow man frequently take God's name in vain? Profanity is the native tongue of the lawless and criminal elements. When all reverence and respect for God fall victim to profanity, disobedience to His other commandments is the next logical step, and almost always follows in due time.

I think it is no accident or coincidence that those who are in the strident forefront of the so-called pro-choice crowd are often known by their loud and angry profanity. The unborn are just as truly image-bearers of God as are their parents, yet when the Lord of life is held in open contempt, so is life itself. In his film *Whatever Happened to the Human Race?*, Dr. Francis Schaeffer pointed out the correlation between loss of reverence for God and loss of respect for human beings as image-bearers. He also warned that the natural development from abortion is infanticide, finally followed by the so-called "good death" of euthanasia.

Is it not time to hear again the somber warning for the man *who taketh his name in vain*?

Question #57: *Which is the fourth commandment?*

Answer: *The fourth commandment is, "Remember the sabbath day, to keep it holy. Six days shalt thou labor and do all thy work: but the seventh day is the sabbath of the Lord thy God: in it thou shalt not do any work, thou, nor thy son, nor thy daughter, thy manservant, nor thy maidservant, nor thy cattle, nor thy stranger that is within thy gates: for in six days the Lord made heaven and earth, the sea, and all that in them is, and rested the seventh day: wherefore the Lord blessed the sabbath day, and hallowed it."*

The Lord Jesus said, *The sabbath was made for man, and not man for the sabbath...it is lawful to do good on the Sabbath.* The fourth commandment teaches us that God has set aside a special day in our lives for Him. This day is made for our good and blessing, and it is to be kept wholly and holy for Him. Jesus' words and His perfect example and interpretation of this commandment provide the key to our understanding of it and obedience to it.

To get some idea of the importance of this commandment, and of this day in the sight of God, please remember that there are only ten commandments. God could have given us ten thousand laws, but He gave us ten. These ten words are very basic and fundamental. They provide the foundation for all law and for the conduct of God's people.

But a strange thing has happened among God's people. It has happened before, and always to the detriment of His people and the diminishing of their influence and testimony. Many in this generation of the church have decided that there are only nine commandments, and this is the one which has been voted out. There have been many attempts lately to prove that God no longer requires obedience to this law. If the same sort of hermeneutical gymnastics were applied to the rest of the commandments, we would be relieved of any responsibility of obedience.

Though this may be the least regarded of all the commandments, it is still the fourth of the list of God's basic laws. In fact, the sabbath law is older than Sinai. It is as old as creation itself. God not only established the sabbath as a part of the creation, but observed it himself by resting on the seventh day. It should come as no surprise, then, to find this law given on the Holy Mount as a part of the basic code of conduct for God's people.

While it is true that in certain eras of history there has been an overly legalistic view of the sabbath, the opposite extreme is just as dangerous and just as harmful to our relationship to the Lord. In the Old Testament the sabbath was to be regarded with delight and joy, but it was to be regarded and taken seriously. God promised His people that if they would honor Him on His day, He would bless them; and, conversely, He warned of sure punishment if they failed to so honor Him.

When the Lord Jesus came to earth, He taught by example and precept that it was right to do good on the sabbath. It was right for him to heal the sick and care for the needy. He allowed His disciples to pluck and eat the grains of wheat in the fields as they went along. So the principle of allowing and even encouraging deeds of mercy and necessity has set the standard for sabbath observance even to this day. If only believers would follow His teachings, there would be little room for controversy and less time for the sinful, selfish pursuits of the world on God's holy day.

Question #58: *What is required in the fourth commandment?*

Answer: *The fourth commandment requireth the keeping holy to God such times as he hath appointed in his word; expressly one whole day in seven to be a holy Sabbath to himself.*

Question #59: *Which day of the seven hath God appointed to be the weekly Sabbath?*

Answer: *From the beginning of the world to the resurrection of Christ, God appointed the seventh day of the week to be the weekly Sabbath; and the first day of the week, ever since, to continue to the end of the world, which is the Christian Sabbath.*

Question #60: *How is the Sabbath to be sanctified?*

Answer: *The Sabbath is to be sanctified by a holy resting all that day, even from such worldly employments and recreations as are lawful on other days; and spending the whole time in the public and private exercises of God's worship, except so much as is to be taken up in the works of necessity and mercy.*

Question #61: *What is forbidden in the fourth commandment?*

Answer: *The fourth commandment forbiddeth the omission, or careless performance, of the duties required, and the profaning the day by idleness, or doing that which is in itself sinful, or by unnecessary thoughts, words, or works, about our worldly employments or recreations.*

Question #62: *What are the reasons annexed to the fourth commandment?*

Answer: *The reasons annexed to the fourth commandment are, God's allowing us six days of the week for our own employments, his challenging a special propriety in the seventh, his own example, and his blessing the Sabbath day.*

The fourth commandment is far older than the ten commandments as given on Mount Sinai. As noted in our last study, God instituted the Sabbath at the dawn of creation. After finishing the magnificent work of creation, God rested on the seventh day and set it aside as a day of rest and as a reminder that this world is a part of the Creator's handiwork, and that man is made in His image.

A question that inevitably comes up is: Why do Christians worship on the first day instead of the seventh? I assume that most if not all who read this will have already had that question answered, but in brief summary, let's state again why this is done. In the very earliest days of the church, believers gathered on the first day of the week for fellowship and worship. The resurrection was the beginning of the new creation, and the gathering for worship was an expression of their joy and faith in the triumph of Christ. Paul's letters to the churches make it clear that this was universal practice in the churches. Not only does Paul speak of believers worshiping on the first day, but John also records in the book of Revelation, *I was in the Spirit on the Lord's day*. This may be seen as an indication that this was the Christian's day of worship. The unbroken history of the church from its first days down to the present bears witness to the acceptance of the transfer of the Sabbath from the seventh to the first day.

Though there may be some minor disagreement on the specific day, there should be none on the principle that God requires one day for Himself to be set aside from the toil and pleasures of this world. What are some of the requirements for keeping the Sabbath? We must be careful not to fall into the error of the Pharisees and try to invent an artificial and extra-Biblical list of do's and don'ts. However, guidelines are in order. God requires worship from His people. This is clearly taught in His Word. Public and corporate worship are essential for the proper keeping of the Sabbath. Service in the name and for the cause of Christ is another positive and proper use of our time on the Lord's day. The example and teaching of Christ on this subject are all we need for motivation and warrant. We may do such deeds as necessity may require and charity demand. Of course, rest is another requirement the commandment specifies.

There are also some "don't" principles. Again, this does not mean a list, but guidelines. First of all, we must avoid the wrong attitude of defiance and selfishness. Instead of defending everything we wish to do on the grounds of Christian liberty, we would do well to simply ask of all our activities, "Does this truly honor God on His day, and does it keep His Sabbath holy?" If we would honestly do this, most of our questions would be answered. One very important don't is this: Don't let popular opinion, even within the church, prevail over the clear teaching of God's Word. Commercialization of the Sabbath is a trap into which many believers have fallen. Clearly God is not pleased with this, any more than He is by the pursuit of selfish pleasures that leave no time to think on the Lord and His goodness. God has given us six days each week to accomplish our work and enjoy our pleasures. He has given us one day for special fellowship with Him, and for rest from our busy lives. He set the example by resting from His labors of creation. He has also given the command to honor Him and His day.

Lo, how our forefathers loved and honored the Sabbath.

More attention is given to this commandment than any of the others. A total of six questions and answers are devoted to the fourth commandment. Isn't it time serious-minded believers of today reclaimed the Sabbath for God?

Question #63: *Which is the fifth commandment?*

Answer: *The fifth commandment is, "Honor thy father and thy mother: that thy days may be long upon the land which the Lord thy God giveth thee."*

The Word of God commands us, *Honor thy father and thy mother,* and, *Children, obey your parents in the Lord, for this is right.* It also says, *Fathers, provoke not your children to wrath, but bring them up in the nurture and admonition of the Lord.* The fifth commandment is the hinge commandment. It stands between the two tables of the law and binds them together, forming a bridge between our duty to God and our duty to man. Obedience to this law will go a long way toward fulfilling the commandments to love God with all our hearts and our neighbors as ourselves.

The purpose of this law is to lay a solid foundation for the family, which is the most basic unit of society and is the model and pattern after which all government is to be formed. This is true not only in the church, but in the civil state as well. The elders in the church are the spiritual fathers of the congregation. Therefore, this commandment applies to them and to the congregation over which they rule. The elected officials in civil government ideally are as fathers to the citizens and live under this law of God, too. Seldom is this ideal achieved; nevertheless, this is God's intention, and civil rulers are answerable to God, who alone gives them authority to rule. Our Lord Jesus Christ reminded godless Pontius Pilate of this reality when He said to him, *Thou couldest have no power at all against me, except if it were given thee from above.*

The survival of true government depends upon the survival

of the family, and the survival of the family depends upon obedience to this law of God. The main reason why we are beginning to see the breakdown of law and order, and the increasing chaos of disorderly and rebellious conduct, is the failure of the American family to function according to this law. The perfect law of God has been replaced by the very imperfect law of Dr. Spock and others like him, and we are paying a dreadful price. The youth rebellion which began in the sixties and the radical feminist movement since that time have both sprung from a rejection of this most fundamental law for an orderly and God-honoring society.

Someone with a gift for poetical expression once said, "My son, all you have on earth you owe to your parents. They have given you life, and thus have given you the privilege of seeing the majesty of the sun, the moon, the stars; the glorious beauty of the snow-capped hills, the blue ocean, and the endless beauty of the changing seasons." God's Word says, *Honor thy father and thy mother*. It is precisely at this point the ten commandments have a unique feature which none of the ancient man-made codes have included. This is a requirement that mothers share equally in the honor and respect children owe their fathers. This reflects very important truths concerning mothers and women in general. First, women are image-bearers of God just as much as men; and secondly, mothers have an equally high place in God's plan for the family, though their roles differ from those of men. In one place where this law is repeated in the Old Testament, the order is reversed, and children are commanded to obey their mothers and their fathers. This places upon the fathers the responsibility to set the example for their children by showing their wives honor and respect. In our next study we will examine more closely what is required and what is forbidden in this commandment.

Question #64: *What is required in the fifth commandment?*

Answer: *The fifth commandment requireth the preserving the honor, and performing the duties, belonging to everyone in their several places and relations, as superiors, inferiors, or equals.*

The catechism makes it quite clear that this law of God not only includes the family unit, but also has much wider application to society as a whole. The catechism is being faithful to Scripture in making this point. The first part of Ephesians 6 elaborates on this and makes the application far beyond simply the family unit.

This law applies to the relationship between employer and employee, between the citizen and the state. By the law we are taught respect for all forms of authority which God may place over us. In I Peter, the Apostle points out that even though government may be unworthy, still it is God's agent of authority and must be obeyed. Of course, there are limits to this, and the attempt to discern those limitations has been a subject of debate and controversy down through history. For instance, both Patriots and Tories quoted Scripture to justify their positions during the American Revolution. In more recent history, believers in Nazi Germany faced many hard choices in their resistance to tyranny. Many pastors, elders, and church members gave their lives protesting the inhuman and ungodly policies of that wicked regime. Others bowed to government pressure and found themselves participating by silent consent in the terrible atrocities associated with mass genocide.

In our own country in more recent years, we saw many youths refusing to register for the draft on the grounds they might have to fight in wars they considered morally wrong. However, at the same time they eagerly accepted government handouts for their education and ignored the ironic contradiction they brought upon themselves.

Let us examine more closely the requirements of this law. First, it teaches the duty of parents to their children. The honor and obedience required of children toward their parents implies a prior duty of the parents to display the character and conduct worthy of that respect and obedience. God requires that parents be spiritual leaders and teachers of their children, both by example and by instruction. When we bring our children for covenant baptism, this responsibility is stressed in the vows we take. Among other things, we promise to set before them a godly example and to instruct them in the Christian faith. When we do this, it is an expression of obedience to this commandment.

One of the often-overlooked and neglected duties of this law is that of godly discipline. Suffice it to say that we are reaping a terrible harvest from our failure at this point.

The other side of this commandment has to do with the duty which children owe their parents. What is this duty? Obedience is the first law of love toward parents and toward God. Jesus said, *If you love me, keep my commandments*. The same thing is true in children's relationships to their parents. If you love your parents, obey them. This is the pathway to honor and respect, and to a right relationship with God. The Bible places disobedience to parents in the same category with murder, theft, witchcraft, and other heinous crimes.

Not only does this law affect the family unit, but many other relations as well. However, a short review of some of the points concerning the family is in order. First, it is significant to note that this commandment includes both parents as objects of honor and obedience. This is unique among all the ancient law codes. In man-made codes, the father alone was accorded this place of honor; but in God's law, the mother shares equally. In fact, when the law is repeated elsewhere in the Old Testament, the order is reversed, and children are commanded to honor their mothers and their fathers. It is the duty of the Christian father to set an example for his children by honoring their mother. Unfortunately, this is not always done.

Another word concerning discipline is necessary as we consider this commandment in the context of the family. Godly discipline is ordained by God, and it is neglected only at terrible cost to the family and to society as a whole. The breakdown of law and order, loss of respect for authority, and moral chaos around us are largely due to the failure of parents to exercise discipline as God's

Word requires. Children who are not properly disciplined by their parents will never learn self-discipline and will become a menace to society. The book of Provers says, *He who spares the rod, hates his child.* How true this is. There are several tragic examples in Scripture.

Three generations of good men failed miserably in this. Eli, the priest, would not discipline his sons for their abuse of the priesthood, and so witnessed their deaths and the end of his lineage. Samuel, sent by God to warn Eli of his failure and terrible consequences to follow, failed to discipline his own sons, who in turn were rejected as leaders in Israel. David, whom Samuel anointed as King, followed in the tragic footsteps of Eli and Samuel.

Discipline means far more than punishment for wrongdoing. It involves instruction and encouragement in right doing. Martin Luther once said to keep both the rod and an apple handy in the training of children. Failure to recognize and reward well-doing is just as destructive as the failure to punish wrong behavior.

In our generation, honoring parents takes on a whole new dimension. People are living much longer than in the past. The care of the elderly is not primarily the responsibility of the government, though many would like for it to be. The foremost responsibility falls upon the children. This may or may not mean that elderly parents live with their children until they die, but it does certainly mean that children must help provide for the care and well-being of the parents when they can no longer care for themselves. This may be costly and complicated, but it must be done. As a pastor, I often visit in nursing homes with elderly people who have not seen their children in years. I once visited a church member whose pastor-son visited her once a year. As with all the commandments, the believer has the responsibility to understand and, more importantly, to obey all the requirements of the fifth commandment.

Question #65: *What is forbidden in the fifth commandment?*

Answer: *The fifth commandment forbiddeth the neglecting of, or doing anything against, the honor and duty which belongeth to everyone in their several places and relations.*

The further development of the teaching of this commandment is brought out in this question and answer. The key words here are *neglecting* and *doing anything against*. Just as the neglect of obedience to any law is breaking that law, so in this one particularly, is neglect of the duty taught to be the most serious form of violation.

Let's begin by looking at this from the perspective of parental duty. This commandment requires of parents that they set a godly example before their children. This automatically forbids an unworthy example. In explaining the reasons for the wickedness of a king of Israel, the Scripture records, *For his mother was his counselor for evil*. What a terrible condemnation! In his case, this was a deliberate attempt by the king's mother to turn him away from the worship of the true God. However, it would be possible for well-meaning parents to become *counselors for evil* by default. Our children learn as much from what they see in us as they do by what they hear from us.

Don't get the wrong idea. A good example, though very important, is not enough. The Bible commands us to teach our children by precept, too. Failure to teach our children the Word of God is a terrible violation of this commandment. Of course, there are many other scriptures which also command to teach them God's Word. We are to teach them of God's love, but we are to warn them that *the wages of sin is death*. We must make very sure we teach them the basic message of the Bible and instruct them in its doctrines. If we neglect to do this, we are breaking this commandment. There is so much more which needs to be said of these things. The failure to love with a godly love that includes discipline is another serious breach of obedience to the fifth commandment.

Now let us look at the duty children owe their parents. In the previous study, we mentioned the sin of disobedience. We noted that the Bible places this sin in the context of the most serious sins we may ever commit. One more thing needs to be said of this. Rebellion against parental authority is rebellion against God. Here again we may see how neglect of parental teaching, and the failure to obey, is just as serious as outright disobedience and rebellion.

Respect is a duty of this commandment, and the lack of respect for parents and other persons in positions of authority is forbidden by this commandment. Jesus Christ, to whom all authority had been given, placed Himself under the authority of His earthly parents. George Washington, who is one of the most respected figures in history, was a man who put great emphasis on respecting his parents' wishes. At one point, he gave up his intended career as a sailor out of respect for his mother's wishes. Needless to say, God greatly honored that respect. Unfortunately, respect for parents, and others in authority, has greatly diminished in these latter days. This is but a symptom of a growing lack of respect for God and His Word.

Finally, we should listen carefully to how this question is posed. What is forbidden in the fifth commandment? It is God who forbids neglect and doing things against the honor and duty owed to parents. *Forbidden* is a serious word which should be taken seriously by serious-minded believers. It is far more than mere suggestion, it is command from God.

Question #66: *What is the reason annexed to the fifth commandment?*

Answer: *The reason annexed to the fifth commandment is, a promise of long life and prosperity (as far as it shall serve for God's glory, and their own good) to all such as keep this commandment.*

There is a passage in Jeremiah 35 which is an excellent commentary on this extraordinary promise which God makes to those who honor Him by honoring their parents. The faithful Rechabites were used of God to rebuke unfaithful Judah for breaking their covenant vows to God. The Rechabites were the descendants of a man who had vowed that neither he nor any of his offspring would ever drink wine. Jeremiah brought them into the house of God and set wine before them, bidding them to drink. Even though Jeremiah was a prophet of God, they refused because of the vow of their father. Jeremiah cited their steadfastness to their father's vow as a rebuke to the men of Judah who had broken their fathers' vows and their own. He said, *They have obeyed their father's command, but I have spoken to you again, and again, and you have not listened to me. Then to the Rechabites God said, Because you have obeyed the command of Jonadab your father, and kept all his commands, …therefore thus says the Lord of Hosts, the God of Israel, Jonadab, son of Rechab, shall not lack a man to stand before me forever.*

God honors those who honor His Word. The continuity of organized society in a large sense depends upon obedience to this law, with all its many implications and applications. Remember the catechism pointed out that this law applies to all in positions of authority and submission. The roots of the fragmentation of our culture with all its many manifestations of lawlessness, lies in the breaking of this vital law which our God has given us. Disobedience to parents and to others in authority, especially those who conscientiously strive to be faithful, is disobedience to God. He is our Father in heaven, and the first duty this law requires is obedience to Him.

Notice how the catechism qualifies this promise. We need to hear this and understand it, and even go a bit beyond what the catechism says. Although this is a law with general application to people, churches, generations, and nations, it is not an unqualified promise of long life on this earth in every individual case. There is indeed a principle here with broad application, but there are exceptions. So far as life on this earth is concerned, it is not always for the good of the believer, nor is it always for the glory of God, that all who obey this command, even within the limits of human possibility, live long lives. We must trust both the wisdom and the goodness of our dear Father in heaven to know and do what is best for His beloved ones. If He calls us home in the tender years of childhood or youth, or in the days of our strength in full manhood or womanhood, or if He allows us long and prosperous days on this earth, it is because in His great love and mercy He is doing for our good what is best.

However, like all the promises of God, this one is not limited to the short days of this life, nor even primarily concerned with them. This is a promise of eternity. Those who honor God, the Father, by trusting in His Son, the Lord Jesus, and therefore seek to honor His precepts and claim His promises, will find that of all the good promises He has made, not one has ever, ever failed.

Question #67: *Which is the sixth commandment?*

Answer: *The sixth commandment is, "Thou shalt not kill."*

Question #68: *What is required in the sixth commandment?*

Answer: *The sixth commandment requireth all lawful endeavors to preserve our own life, and the life of others.*

This commandment from God is very straightforward and direct. *Thou shalt not kill.* It teaches the sacredness of life and forbids the terrible sin of murder and all related sins. We live in a world and a time when this law is ignored to a shocking extent. In the eyes of many, human life is dreadfully cheap. For a handful of change, a street criminal kills his victim. Thousands die in drug-related crimes. Moreover, there is widespread indifference to such events. But God never revokes His commandment.

When this law was given, it was sorely needed. The tragedy of Cain and Abel had long been forgotten. God's commandment to Noah, *Whoso sheds man's blood, by man shall his blood be shed*, had been laid aside. As it is now, so it was then: life was cheap. Moses, through whom this law was given, barely escaped with his life while still a helpless infant. Pharaoh had decreed that all male babies of the Hebrews were to be thrown into the Nile. Only the faith and courage of Moses' parents saved his life.

But is that shocking scene of infanticide any more terrible than the wholesale slaughter of the unborn in our own country? In the age of Moses, a master could kill his slave without accounting for the act. Fathers had life-and-death power over their children. Kings killed messengers who brought bad news. The ancient world desperately needed to hear God thunder from Mount Sinai, *Thou shalt not kill.* Is our modern world in any less need of this law? Recently venerable Princeton University, once a strong fortress of Biblical Christianity (but no more) employed a professor who openly advocates the murder of handicapped children by their parents. Moreover, he is defended in his hideous philosophy by the university.

Who are we to cast stones at another era? Our own indifference to human life in undeniable. We are so accustomed to violent death, we become immune to shock. Recently, a young man was killed while serving a prison sentence for a fairly minor offense. Public reaction was less than overwhelming. The only comment I heard was, "He got what he deserved. He shouldn't have been in prison in the first place."

Much of our concern in the Christian world for human life is limited by fads. Of course, we are all very upset about mass abortion. Yet, many Christian students admit to alcohol abuse, despite the fact that over 10,000 people are killed every year by drunken drivers. Many of the same students, however, are very vocal in their opposition to abortion. Some churches hold all-night vigils against capital punishment, but how often do you hear of these churches holding vigils for families of victims of murderers?

How may we as Christians obey this law? The answer must include obedience to the spirit of the law as well as the letter. Above all, the basic teaching of this commandment is summed up in these words, *I am my brother's keeper.* I am responsible for his life and well-being. Life is a sacred trust from God – both my own life and my neighbor's. Therefore, I must take all reasonable steps to preserve his life and mine. This commandment requires me to do all I can to express this responsibility to those around me. It also requires that I support laws designed to protect and defend life. Obedience to this law means I must support punishment of those who break it, and defend innocent victims.

There is, however, yet a higher duty in this commandment. According to the Bible, life in its fullest expression is a right relationship to God. We must never forget that all people apart from this saving relationship through Jesus Christ are under sentence of death. So, as a believer, I must do everything in my power to spread the good news of the Gospel to all men everywhere. We would all rise up and condemn a doctor who refused to treat a dying person. How much more reprehensible for Christians to ignore those who are spiritually dead and withhold the only cure for their condition? The God who said, *Thou shalt not kill*, commands us to preach the Gospel to all the world.

Question #69: *What is forbidden in the sixth commandment?*

Answer: *The sixth commandment forbiddeth the taking away of our own life, or the life of our neighbor unjustly, or whatsoever tendeth thereunto.*

The most obvious sin this commandment forbids is that of outright, premeditated murder. Long before this commandment was formally given, men knew that it was wrong and sinful to murder. Cain was the first murderer, and he was held accountable before God and man for his foul deed. Cain ignored God's warning and was overcome by the sin crouched at the door of his heart.

When God began again with Noah and gave the fundamental laws which were to guide and govern the human race after the flood, a law concerning murder was one of the most prominent of these precepts. *Whoever sheddeth man's blood, by man shall his blood be shed*. This law is an absolute necessity for the preservation of law and order, and the protection of human life. Unfortunately, we have decided we are smarter than God and have all but eliminated this law. Even in states which still practice capital punishment, so many restrictions have been added as to make the law of little effect. And what a price we have paid, and will yet pay, for our disobedience. Murder, the sin expressly forbidden in this law, runs wild in our nation. Thousands fall victim to this crime every year, but our society seems more interested in protecting the rights of convicted murderers than in protecting the lives of their victims. When will we ever learn that God knows best?

This law also deals with sins which lead to murder. It is certainly possible to break this law by neglect and indifference. If I know that my neighbor is in great danger and do nothing about it, I have broken this law. If I were to see my neighbor's house afire and fail to warn him, or attempt rescue, would I not be guilty of breaking this commandment? There are so many other ways in which we may violate this law. The person who drives in a deliberately careless manner, ignoring the laws of safety and speed, or who drives while under the influence of drugs or alcohol may cause the death of another.

A young high school girl was the victim of careless gossip by some of her classmates. They told tales which implied that she was sexually promiscuous. Unfortunately, these lies were believed by many. She was so distraught that she finally took her own life, rather than face the taunts of her classmates. Although nothing was done to the gossips, other than a severe lecture, surely in God's sight they had broken the sixth commandment. As a matter of fact, she had, too, for this law forbids suicide.

Jesus used this law to show how one must obey not only the letter but the spirit of the law as well. According to Christ, anger, hatred, contempt may lead to murder and are a violation of this law. He sternly warned against these attitudes which break the spirit of God's law. Behind the angry hatred of another person lies the sin of an unforgiving heart. This blocks the work of the Spirit in your life and leaves you open to the Devil's deadly work. There are other slippery steps which may lead to murder. Envy, resentment, revenge, and retaliation are dangerous attitudes, and quickly dominate the thinking of one who surrenders to their influence. Indeed, most murders grow out of one of these four sins.

Surely we must recognize that we are a nation guilty of murder on a mass scale, when we think of the horror of mass abortion, the growing acceptance of infanticide, and so-called euthanasia. As believers we must not only guard our own lives against any of the sins forbidden by the sixth commandment, but also join with others in resisting the rising tide of disobedience to this fundamental law God gave us to preserve and protect human life.

Question #70: *Which is the seventh commandment?*

Answer: *The seventh commandment is, "Thou shalt not commit adultery."*

There is a verse of poetry from James Russell Lowell which goes like this:

> *In vain we call old notions fudge*
> *and bend our conscience to our dealing;*
> *The ten commandments will not budge,*
> *and stealing will continue stealing.*

And adultery will continue to be adultery.

In spite of all our frantic efforts to ignore or negate this commandment of God, it remains, unchanged and powerful. Let me remind you again of a principle of interpretation in understanding the commandments. The purpose of God's law is not to be understood as a code which prevents or forbids the fulfillment of our human nature. We are not even to think of them as a list of do's and don'ts. Rather, they are God's guideposts pointing in the direction of true fulfillment and ultimate joy. None of the commandments illustrate this principle more clearly than the seventh, *Thou shalt not commit adultery*. For all the sins forbidden by this commandment seem to offer happiness, freedom, contentment, and fulfillment. Deluded by these false hopes, modern man has abandoned this law and embraced all forms of immorality as an acceptable way of life.

So what do we find? Rather than being able to fulfill all these apparent promises, this way of life leads to misery, bondage, and living death. Furthermore, they separate us from the true source and meaning of love: God.

If one of the primary purposes of the law is to convict of sin, this is one law which should bring us all to our knees, in sincere repentance, with a cry for mercy. Is there any one of God's laws more rejected and flaunted than this one? Is there any law more necessary for modern man to hear? But because he will not hear it, and because he will ignore it, modern man is trapped in the chains of self-imposed bondage.

Any discussion of morality or marriage must begin with this commandment. Any study of human sexuality should begin at this point. All relationships between members of the opposite sex should be guided first of all by this commandment. There is a crying need for believers to become the light of the world and the salt of the earth at this point. Unfortunately, this is not always the case. The light of many believers no longer shines brightly with purity and steadfastness. We have been conformed to the world. Even if we have escaped the actual overt sins associated with this commandment, we have absorbed much of the lascivious lifestyle of the unregenerate. Yet believers committed to personal purity are the only ones who offer any hope of any light to guide people out of the darkness of immorality. If believers compromise the truth at this point, we serve only to increase the darkness and hopelessness of humanity.

As one begins to consider the terrifying statistics of broken homes, ruined marriages, blighted lives, confused and abused children, not to mention such horrors as venereal diseases, AIDS, teen pregnancies, rape, and other sexual crimes, it is truly appalling. What lies at the root of these problems? The rejection of God's law, which says, *Thou shalt not commit adultery*. God refuses to accommodate His standards to the changing ideas and ideals of fallen man. It is past time for believers to join in this refusal, and to rededicate ourselves to obedience in act and thought to this command.

Question #71: *What is required in the seventh commandment?*

Answer: *The seventh commandment requireth the preservation of our own and our neighbor's chastity, in heart, speech, and behavior.*

Question #72: *What is forbidden in the seventh commandment?*

Answer: *The seventh commandment forbiddeth all unchaste thoughts, words, and actions.*

When a commandment from our God begins with *Thou shalt not*, we may make the mistake of assuming there is only a negative emphasis in such a command. The catechism rightly poses the question, *What is required?*, before it deals with *What is forbidden?* In dealing with the touchy and sensitive issues surrounding the seventh commandment, it is well to begin with the most positive of all exhortations we find in Scripture. *Husbands love your wives as Christ loved the church...wives be in subjection to your own husbands as unto the Lord.* What could be more positive than this? What better place to begin to explore the requirements of this command? Obedience to these words from Ephesians would go far in fulfilling the seventh commandment. If a man loves his wife in the way that Christ loved the church, and gave Himself up for it, there would be no room in his life for anyone else to share that kind of love. Even the temptations in this area to which all are subject, would lose much of their power.

As for the wife, especially one who is blessed by this kind of loving and self-sacrificing husband, her submission to her own husband would eliminate the desire to be in submission to any other man. As she understood that submission to her husband was simply a part of her submission to the Lord, the yoke would be easy and the burden light.

Philippians 4:8 speaks of the positive requirements of this law. *Finally brethren whatever things are true, whatever things are noble, whatever things are just, whatever things are pure, whatever things are lovely, whatever things are of good report, if there is any virtue, and if there is anything praiseworthy – meditate on these things.* This sort of Christ-controlled thinking will guard the mind against the impure thought, the temptations towards unchaste actions, and the overwhelming desires of our fallen nature. It is never enough to say no to these things. We must say yes to purity in thought, word, and deed.

The words of Jesus also come to mind when He was asked, *What is the first and great commandment?* His answer, quoting from Deuteronomy, was, *You shall love the Lord your God with all your heart, with all your soul, and with all your strength.* Then he added, *...you shall love your neighbor as yourself. Upon these two commandments hang all the law and the prophets.* In short, he was teaching us (among other things) that obedience to the seventh commandment, as well as all others, is summed up in loving God with all your heart, and your neighbor as yourself. This is truly what is required in the seventh commandment.

The sins forbidden by this commandment are stated in some detail in the Larger Catechism. As you study that list you will discover a dismal catalog of the very actions and thoughts that are glorified in our corrupt contemporary culture. Beware, believers! All too many professing Christians are joining in the approval (and practice) of the many sins which fall under the condemnation of God's Word. Those who speak out against such terrible sins such as adultery, fornication, rape, incest, homosexuality, and all contributing causes are now the villains of our society.

Christians just don't seem to understand that when you engage in all the sinful pleasures and tendencies of our culture; reading and watching what the ungodly read and watch; dressing and talking as the ungodly dress and talk; that you will end up behaving as the ungodly behave. Hear these words and hear them well, *The wrath of God is revealed against all ungodliness...*

The consequences of participating in the sins forbidden by this commandment are seen all around us. Vulgarity in speech has become commonplace. Crimes of sexual violence, especially against the weak and helpless, such as young children, have multiplied beyond our worst fears. The church's timidity in taking a strong Biblical stand on such issues as unlawful marriages and unlawful divorces is undermining not only the church itself, but the home as well. I have been appalled and amazed in recent years to realize how much more time I now spend in counseling Christians in troubled marriages, as compared with the time spent in this same ministry only a few years ago. The anger, resentment, confusion, and hatred of children against their parents and step-parents are understandable, but alarming and devastating.

There is good reason why God forbids the many sins associated with the seventh commandment. These things dishonor God and corrupt human nature, and they are destructive of Christian witness in a world of darkness and despair.

Question #73: *Which is the eighth commandment?*

Answer: *The eighth commandment is, "Thou shalt not steal."*

The sin of stealing has become a national epidemic and a national disgrace. It is undermining our whole social and economic fabric; yet theft, along with all of its associated sins of dishonesty, has become so deeply ingrained into our way of life that many may be guilty of breaking this commandment without fully realizing they are doing so.

It would be possible simply to list many ways in which this commandment is broken and fill page after page. However, I will not do this lest I give you ideas you don't need. Though I do not have actual statistics, it is safe to say that stealing is the most commonly committed crime worldwide. It lies at the root of many other crimes, especially crimes of violence leading to injury and loss of life. Armed robbery has become so commonplace, it scarcely deserves an item in the newspaper. However, if you read any newspaper in any city in America on any day, you will read at least one account of armed robbery and this account will probably include serious injury or death for the victims of the robbery.

There are many other forms of stealing which violate God's commandment. For example, a few years back there was a serious snowstorm in the Southeast. This storm left many thousands of travelers stranded on interstate highways. It was reported that in and around Atlanta the price of motel and hotel rooms doubled, tripled, and in some cases increased even more. Thousands of people paid unheard-of prices for refuge from the storm. Taking advantage of people in such situations is obviously stealing. In fact, the Larger Catechism mentions this as one form of violating the eighth commandment.

Do you realize that hundreds of small businesses are forced into bankruptcy because of stealing? Ordinarily, this is done by the employees of the company, or it may be simply in the form of shoplifting. Or it may take the form of customers refusing to pay their debts. I recently talked with a businessman who had been forced to close his business because the U.S. Government was so long in paying the bills he submitted.

There is another symptom of the national epidemic which deserves mention. Many criminals who are apprehended are never prosecuted. There is a system called plea bargaining by which some are allowed to plead guilty to a lesser crime to avoid being prosecuted for stealing. When there are riots in major cities, one of the first things that happens is that people take to the streets and break into shops and stores, stealing anything that may be carried away. They are seldom if ever prosecuted. In fact, such behavior is sometimes justified with the excuse that they are underprivileged and are expressing their frustrations. Because we reject any absolute standard of right or wrong, including the eighth commandment, we have developed an ethic which excuses criminal action on the basis of need, real or imaginary. I fail to see how a stolen television set really meets a legitimate need.

Now we are living in an era when technology has made it possible and relatively simple to commit major theft by electronic manipulation. This is usually referred to as white-collar crime, yet the criminal is just as guilty as the thug on the street who threatens his victim with gun or knife. Time would fail us to tell of the savings and loan disaster which threatened to wreck our whole economic structure. The evidence at this point suggested that over a trillion dollars had been misappropriated through these now bankrupt institutions.

Next we will try to consider some ways in which we may be obedient to this law and thus fulfill the intention behind it.

Question #74: *What is required in the eighth commandment?*

Answer: *The eighth commandment requireth the lawful procuring and furthering the wealth and outward estate of ourselves and others.*

Question #75: *What is forbidden in the eighth commandment?*

Answer: *The eighth commandment forbiddeth whatsoever doth, or may, unjustly hinder our own or our neighbor's wealth or outward estate.*

The eighth commandment, which in the Hebrew literally says, "No stealing," is rooted in the nature of man created in God's image. God is the ultimate owner of all things. The whole earth and all of its resources and all of its people belong to God. When God created man in His own image, he entrusted him with the stewardship of possessions. He conferred upon man the right of possession and built into the very fabric of creation the right to own, control, and use property and material wealth. Because of this it is a sin against God for me to take what God entrusted to you.

Man in his relationship to God can never claim absolute ownership of anything. Man in his relationship to man, however, has been given the right and responsibility of ownership. It therefore becomes our duty to possess, control, and use all our material wealth to the glory of God and for the benefit of ourselves and others. By implication, this commandment forbids that we should take from another any of his possessions unless our labor earns it or his love confers it.

This commandment also forbids that I should even desire to take whatever belongs to other people. So there is a very close correlation between this commandment and the tenth which says, *Thou shalt not covet.* As a matter of fact, coveting usually leads to stealing in one form or another.

In the fourth chapter of Ephesians, the Apostle lays down a general pattern of honest living and then speaks quite specifically to the matter of stealing. He says, *Let him that stole steal no more: but rather let him labor, working with his hands the thing which is good, that he may have to give to him that needeth.* Of course, from this there are many other implications concerning our obedience to this commandment. According to Scripture, dishonest business actions are a form of stealing. In fact, it is surprising to discover how many of the writings of the Old Testament prophets deal with just weights and dishonest scales. The dishonest use of scales and balances is listed with such serious sins as murder and kidnapping and idolatry.

The Bible also warns against defrauding the laborer of his wages. In Deuteronomy 24 we are told that if a poor man works for you, you must pay him that very day, lest he go hungry and have no place to sleep. The book of James warns that on the day of judgment the testimony of the laborer who has been denied his just wages will be held against the rich man.

The other side is that the worker may defraud the employer by failing to give an honest day's work for a day's wages. We cannot escape the fact that God is intensely concerned with simple, basic honesty. Our profession must mean more than just attending church or Bible studies or prayer meetings. These things are important, but they must lead us to practice godliness and honesty in the world in which we live.

One further comment on this commandment is in order. On a national level, we have pursued an economic policy that places intolerable burdens of dept upon succeeding generations. We are in effect requiring them to pay for our greed. Surely this is a form of stealing and is one reason why God's hand of judgment seems to be on our nation with all its economic problems. If we find ourselves guilty of breaking this commandment in any of the many forms suggested, our first step is repentance and our second step is obedience, including restitution where appropriate. And it is required of believers to take these steps if they are to walk in the way of the Lord.

Question #76: *Which is the ninth commandment?*

Answer: *The ninth commandment is, "Thou shalt not bear false witness against thy neighbor."*

The ninth commandment forbids bearing false witness and it requires commitment to the truth. More than we like to admit, our attitude toward this commandment goes something like this: If you lie to me, that is unforgivable; but if I lie to you, that is understandable. If I accuse you of lying, you ought to be ashamed; but if you accuse me of lying (even if I am guilty), it is a terrible offense.

The difference between an ordinary lie and a little white lie is whether I tell it or you tell it. But God sees all lying as just that, and He forbids it by this commandment. Actually, there are many, many places in the Bible which speak of God's dislike of lying. Some of these are as follows: *The Lord hates a lying tongue* (Proverbs 6:17); *He who tells lies shall not abide in my presence* (Psalm 101:7); *Put away lying and speak the truth* (Ephesians 4:25). Some of the most dreadful words of condemnation in the Bible are words which God speaks against false prophets who speak falsehoods in the name of God.

Obedience to this commandment requires an enthusiastic love for the truth as well as hatred for falsehood. Christians all too often excuse themselves from obedience to this commandment and regard it as one of the lesser requirements for Godly living. Would you like to bring discord and strife and misunderstanding to break another person's career or reputation? All you have to do to accomplish these terrible things is to bear false witness, either by outright lies or implications and insinuations, or even simply by failing to tell the truth. Yes, you can accomplish all of this by disobedience to this commandment, but in doing so you will make it impossible to have a loving, trusting relationship with the Lord. This commandment is so basic to your own character that you really need to understand this law, repent of breaking it, and make a heartfelt commitment to keep it.

Like stealing, lying has become so deeply ingrained in our whole way of life that it is difficult to avoid this sin. In fact, it has become difficult for many people to know the difference between the truth and a lie. The father of our nation, George Washington, was quoted as saying, *I cannot tell a lie*. Some of his successors could not tell the truth. Some modern-day politicians seem to say, *I don't know the difference*. Most of us would agree that lying is sinful and dangerous to all concerned, but we tend to make personal exceptions. *I would never tell a lie except to protect myself or make a sale or keep from being fired or maybe to cover another lie.*

There is another problem we face as we attempt to practice obedience to this law. We are living in a time in which most people reject the idea of absolute standards of right and wrong, of truth and falsehood. The humanist contends that what is true today may not be true tomorrow. He believes that what is true for him may not be true for you. This subjective approach to truth undermines the foundations of integrity and honesty. Moreover, people have discovered that if a lie is made to sound convincing and can be repeated often enough, it will be accepted as the truth. This was the ethic of both the Nazis and the Communists in their drives to dominate the world. They came dangerously near succeeding. Unfortunately, it is rapidly becoming the ethic of our own country, which played such a major role in the defeat of these two false ideologies. Will we too fall because of the same sin?

Question #77: *What is required in the ninth commandment?*

Answer: *The ninth commandment requireth the maintaining and promoting of truth between man and man, and of our own and of our neighbor's good name, especially in witness-bearing.*

Question #78: *What is forbidden in the ninth commandment?*

Answer: *The ninth commandment forbiddeth whatsoever is prejudicial to truth, or injurious to our own or our neighbor's good name.*

What are the requirements for obedience to this commandment? What does God expect of His redeemed people?

If you really want to understand this commandment, you must approach it positively. It is above all else a commandment to speak the truth. Although there is a warning implied, it is to be thought of as a teaching what is right in speaking.

It is possible to break this law by guilty silence. If we keep quiet when God commands us to speak the truth, then we have broken the commandment. We must also be careful how we speak the truth. It is possible to take part of the truth and turn it into a lie, and this is often done. It is rightly said that a half-truth is the most dangerous form of a lie.

This law teaches us that God has given us the priceless gift of speech. How we use this gift is very important. We must use it to promote the good of our neighbor by proper speaking of the truth and by refraining from false witnessing. We must protect our neighbor's good name and reputation. We must stand against error and resist evil speech and malicious tale-bearing. If we listen to idle and hurtful gossip in silence, we contribute to its spread and violate this commandment. Our use of the gift of speech should lead us to promote unity and understanding between people.

This law requires that we make promises and keep them. A good example of this would be the vows we take to God in the church when we become members. Another example would be a minister talking to a pulpit committee. It would be required of him to communicate honestly with the committee about his strengths as well as his weaknesses.

If we are to be faithful to this commandment, we are to speak the truth about Jesus Christ and His saving Gospel. This is the greatest truth we know and the best of all good news. If we fail to share that good news with others, we violate the ninth commandment. Of course, this places on us an additional responsibility of living out our profession so the words we speak ring true. A good question we might all ask at this point is: Are you able and willing to share the Gospel with others?

If you are seeking a perfect example of how to obey this law, look to the Lord Jesus Christ. His whole life was one of truthfulness and kindness. Think how He used the gift of speech. *Thy sins be forgiven thee . . . rise up and walk . . . Father, forgive them for they know not what they do.* Truly our Lord Jesus has the words of eternal life. By His words He gave help and hope. He caused light to shine in darkness and drove away falsehood. Even when it cost Him His life, He spoke the truth, saying, *I am the Christ*. The words which cost His life bring life to millions who believe His confession and accept Him as the way, the truth, and the life.

What does this law forbid? It forbids bearing false witness against our neighbor. The book of James has much to say about the wrong use of speech and the seriousness of sinning with our lips. James says that the tongue is tied to the heart and reveals the true condition of a person. He said the tongue is like the rudder of a ship guiding its course, or like a spark that sets off a great flame. Since we are children of a God who is truth itself, obedience to this law becomes a part of our basic testimony.

Question #79: *Which is the tenth commandment?*

Answer: *The tenth commandment is, "Thou shalt not covet thy neighbour's house, thou shalt not covet thy neighbour's wife, nor his manservant, nor his maidservant, nor his ox, nor his ass, nor any thing that is thy neighbour's.*

The first commandment, *Thou shalt have no other gods before me*, and the last commandment, *Thou shalt not covet*, are very closely akin. They deal with the same basic aspect of human nature, though from differing perspectives. The Apostle Paul warns us, *Flee from covetousness which is idolatry*. So in effect the commandments end where they begin. Have you ever tried to analyze the present world in which we live, to determine what lies behind the spirit of unrest which grips all humanity? Why is there an uneasy feeling of disquiet that infects the whole human race? Why is there a government-in-exile of terrorism throughout the whole earth which threatens international chaos? Why are we in the grips of a growing epidemic of violent crime which has become a personal threat to each one of us? Why is it that in almost every neighborhood it has become necessary to have some form of burglar insurance – perhaps an elaborate electronic device or at the very least a loud and obnoxious dog? Why is our national economy in shambles with deficits over $100 billion a year and our budget completely out of control? Why does our national debt number in the trillions of dollars? Why have large corporations become so impersonal, treating their employees as if they were robots and casting aside those who have given years of faithful service as if they were no more than worn-out machines?

The answer to all of these questions lies in one word: covetousness – the all-pervasive sin of human nature. In 10,000 valleys, upon countless green hilltops, under many shady groves, and in the fathomless depths of every ocean lie the bodies of the best young men of almost every generation who have been killed in the mad struggle between warring nations. Behind all of these wars there is the passion to possess, the desire for more.

The sin of greed is so basic to human nature that no one is free from its demanding grasp. It is certainly the prevailing spirit of our present generation, perhaps more than any other. We are in bondage to covetousness. It is a self-imposed bondage, but one from which we are powerless to free ourselves.

Nevertheless, the commandment of God remains unchanged: Thou shalt not covet. It towers over the greed of humanity and the wreckage of human history. It condemns our madness to possess things and offers a more noble way of life.

The last of the ten commandments is unique, for it searches out the spirit of a man rather than his deeds. It does not say so much what you should or should not do as what you should or should not be. It deals with your heart more than any other commandment. This was the commandment which convicted Saul, who was to become Paul, of his sin and lost condition. He said in one place that he was unaware of sin and was not convicted of his sinfulness until he dealt with this commandment. It reached out and slew him and so brought him under bondage to the whole law, exposing his sinful nature and leaving him defenseless in the presence of our holy God.

This commandment, *Thou shalt not covet*, is used by the Holy Spirit even to this day to bring men and women to their knees in recognition and confession of sin. The greatest disgrace in the church of our generation is not so much the immorality of its people and pastors (as serious as this is). No, the great shame is the near-surrender to the sin of covetousness. May God through Christ set us free from this terrible bondage.

Question #80: *What is required in the tenth commandment?*

Answer: *The tenth commandment requireth full contentment with our condition, with a right and charitable frame of spirit toward our neighbor, and all that is his.*

Question #81: *What is forbidden in the tenth commandment?*

Answer: *The tenth commandment forbiddeth all discontentment with our own estate, envying or grieving at the good of our neighbor, and all inordinate motions and affections to anything that is his.*

This commandment has rightly been labeled the catch-all commandment, for it catches us all and spares no one. It tells us we are sinful both by nature and by choice. Even if we could claim a surface obedience to all the other commandments, when we come to this one, we find ourselves unable to defend our innocence.

The sin of covetousness lies at the root of all disobedience. It was at the root of the fall of Adam and Eve in the garden. When Eve saw that the fruit of the tree in the midst of the garden was good for food, pleasant to the eye, and to be desired to make one wise, she ate of it and give it to Adam, and he ate. Their covetousness led to their disobedience. Once again, the connection between the first and the last commandments becomes obvious, for we cannot love God with all our heart and at the same time covet all else.

What does it mean to covet? In the neutral sense of the word, it simply means to strongly desire. But when that desire is misdirected or when it becomes our master, then it is sinful, and we are guilty of that sin.

This law not only forbids covetousness, but forbids the outward expression of it. Another expression of covetousness is the desire for something for nothing. We want reward without effort and this, too, is wrong.

There is a deeper meaning to this commandment. It forbids a worldly spirit that believes that life consists in the abundance of things one possesses. Jesus warned about this when He said, *Beware and take heed of covetousness for life does not consist of the abundance of things that one possesses.* He went on to tell the parable of the rich fool, in which He pointed out the danger of covetousness. Here we discover how covetousness erodes the character of a person, distorts his values, and in the end brings death and ruin.

Jesus also taught by His rebuke of Satan's temptation that man does not live by bread alone. He has a deeper and more urgent need: a right relationship with God. Do you know the one thing the covetous person wants? It's a four-letter word spelled m-o-r-e – more of anything and everything. That kind of covetousness makes contentment impossible. The constant desire to posses more and the lack of contentment add up to misery of the worst sort. The covetous person never knows peace within or with God.

The ultimate outcome of covetousness is seen in the life and death of Judas Iscariot. I'm sure Judas never intended to betray Christ when he first began to desire more worldly possessions. He did not set out to be remembered as the most infamous man in history. All he wanted was just a little more than what he had, but gradually that desire possessed him, until he betrayed Christ and killed himself.

In my own life I have found only one thing effective in overcoming the sin of greed, and that is the faithful practice of stewardship. The more I give, the less hold the things of the world have on me. When I forget and start holding on and trying for more, I find myself a willing captive of covetousness. Once you learn to put God first in a tangible way by tithing and giving offerings above the tithe, the stranglehold of covetousness is loosened and finally broken. The joy and fulfillment of giving replace the captivity of keeping. As you learn more of the grace of gratitude for that which God has placed in your care to be used for His glory, the things of the world have less hold on your heart. It boils down to a choice: either you will conquer the sin of covetousness or it will conquer you, an unthinkable thing for the child of the King.

Question #82: *Is any man able perfectly to keep the commandments of God?*

Answer: *No mere man, since the fall, is able, in this life, perfectly to keep the commandments of God; but doth daily break them, in thought, word, and deed.*

One of the basic points of disagreement even among Christians is this question: Is anyone able to perfectly keep the commandments of God? In giving the negative answer to this, our catechism takes seriously the Biblical teaching of the fall of man and the results of that fall in every area of his life.

There are many people who believe that mankind is basically good and that given the opportunity and the right environment, people will always do the right thing. On the other hand, there are those who believe that human nature is neutral, neither good nor bad, and that training and environment will determine whether the person is good or bad.

The Biblical position is quite clear. When our first parents sinned, there was a fundamental change in human nature. Until that time, Adam and Eve loved God with all their hearts and were able to obey His Word and to live in perfect harmony with Him. In the garden before the fall, human nature was indeed good because our first parents were created in God's image. However, once sin entered into the world, that nature was changed and became totally affected by sin.

One of the five points of Calvinism is *Total Depravity*. Total depravity does not mean that everyone is equally and totally evil. It does mean that our whole nature is affected by sin and that no mere man is able to perfectly keep the commandments of God. The Apostle Paul talks about this in the book of Romans, showing how it is impossible for anyone to be righteous in God's sight through obedience to the law. Paul himself was a willing victim of this inability and spoke of his own frustration in trying to achieve righteousness through the law.

The catechism tells us that we daily break the commandments

of God in thought, word, and deed. This is most clearly taught in our Lord's exposition of the ten commandments contained in the Sermon on the Mount. His summary of the requirements of the law was this, *Be ye therefore perfect even as your Father in heaven is perfect*. However, before making that statement, He took several of the commandments and gave the traditional interpretation and then went on to show the full meaning of obedience to these commandments. In each of these He dealt with obedience from the heart and showed very clearly that no one is capable of obeying the law in thought, word, or deed.

If we fail to understand the importance of this truth, we are led into many areas of error. First of all, we could be tempted to think that we could earn our own salvation by obedience to God's law. It always surprises me how many people really believe this. Yet, to follow this pathway is to experience unending frustration and disappointment that will lead to despair and hopelessness.

Another danger is that we will simply fail to take sin seriously. If I believe that I am able to obey the law of God and yet see myself continually breaking it, I am tempted to rationalize my actions by believing that my failure is not serious or that what I am doing is not wrong at all. This is insulting to God, as it leads us to question His authority, wisdom, and holiness. If I take seriously what the catechism teaches at this point, I will also take seriously the doctrine of grace; and if I take that seriously, then I understand my salvation is rooted in God's purpose and electing grace.

One final word is in order. Those who understand the inability of man to win his own salvation will inevitably strive to obey the law of God out of gratitude and so come nearer meeting its requirements.

Question #83: *Are all transgressions of the law equally heinous?*

Answer: *Some sins in themselves, and by reason of several aggravations, are more heinous in the sight of God than others.*

The best commentary on this question of the Shorter Catechism is to be found in the Larger Catechism in question and answer 151, which really tell us why this statement in the Shorter Catechism is valid. Since most of you will not have read this for yourselves, I will use it as an outline for my brief commentary.

First of all, let it be said that we reject the idea of the classification of sins as mortal and venial, because every sin is deadly. As someone has said, even the slightest sin is cosmic treason against the God of the universe.

However, it is true that for several reasons some sins are more heinous in God's sight than others. What are these reasons? First there is the matter of the person who is offending. It is one thing for a baby Christian to stumble and fall, but it is more serious when a mature Christian does the same thing. The reason for this is clear: the young Christian has not had the benefit of long years of Bible study and prayer and the inner working of the Holy Spirit. On the other hand, the Christian who has had the benefit of all these things has greater responsibility to obey God in thought, word, and deed. Another consideration at this point is that a more mature Christian usually has a wider influence on other people. That is one reason why the Apostle Paul rebuked the Apostle Peter in the presence of the whole assembly. Peter's offense had a detrimental effect on the whole church because of his position of leadership.

This leads us to the second reason why some sins are more serious than others. We have to consider those who are injured by the sin. God is always offended by every sin, but sins that are directed toward Him are even more offensive. An example of this would be blasphemy. On the other hand, sins against weaker believers are also especially serious. When we cause weak Christians to fall by our conduct, then we have violated one of the commands of Scripture, namely, that we avoid offending weaker brothers in the faith. Even in the world, this sort of classification is recognized. Everyone abhors murder, but when the victim is a weak and defenseless person, it is regarded as being even more horrible. In fact, in the matter of capital punishment, this is often taken into consideration.

The third reason why some sins are more heinous in the sight of God than others is the nature of the sin itself. It is a serious sin if in my heart I harbor hate against my brother, but if this hatred breaks out into violence, then the sin is complicated and becomes even more reprehensible. It is wrong for me to covet my neighbor's property, but if I steal that which I covet, I have complicated the offense. If I am overtaken by a sudden temptation this is serious enough, but if I do the same ill deed deliberately, willfully, and maliciously, then it is even worse.

The final "aggravation" that the Larger Catechism mentions is the circumstance of time and place. If the offense is on the Lord's Day, or during worship, that aggravates the sin. Another aspect of this would be whether the sin is public or private. Obviously, the consequences of public sin are much more widely spread and, therefore, more disastrous.

As we shall see in the next question of the catechism, all sins make us liable to God's judgment, but in the Christian life, it is important to realize that there are complicated factors that make some sins more offensive than others. If this study does nothing else, it will remind us how dependent we are on the grace of God and how impossible it is to please Him in our own strength.

Question #84: *What doth every sin deserve?*

Answer: *Every sin deserveth God's wrath and curse, both in this life, and that which is to come.*

This statement from the catechism will probably sound extreme to many who hear and read it. However, a little serious consideration will help you to understand that there is nothing extreme or unbiblical at all about these words. In fact, the Larger Catechism inserts the expression: *even the least*.

Now, why is this true? First of all, we have to understand that all sin is sin against God. When David had committed the terrible sin of murder, his prayer was, *against thee, thee only have I sinned and done this evil in thy sight.* Sin is always against God and His goodness and love. When we break His laws, we break His heart. This makes it a personal offense. It is only as we understand something of God's holiness and goodness that we can begin to comprehend the seriousness of sin.

Moreover, God has given us a very clear pattern in His word of acceptable conduct. We call this the Ten Commandments. It might well be said that much of what the Bible features is a commentary on these ten words. When we say that every sin deserves God's wrath and curse, we are recognizing something about the character of God that is often overlooked. God is a God of righteousness and compassion. It simply shows another side of His character. Since we have every reason for obeying Him and none for disobeying Him, we therefore must reckon with His wrath when we sin against Him. The wrath of God does not mean that God gets mad at people. It does mean that God's wrath is constantly against sin and must be taken seriously.

If there is one place in all the Bible that reveals this side of God's character, it is in the accounts given of Christ's death on the cross. Here we see both the love and the wrath of God in proper balance. God's love sent His Son into the world to bear our sin, and when He took to Himself our sin, God's wrath was poured out on Him. The Apostle Paul said of Christ, *He was made sin for us.* This enables us to understand His heart cry from the cross, *My God, my God, why hast thou forsaken me?* Any time we are tempted to think lightly of our sin, we need to be reminded of that dreaded scene on Calvary's hill.

The catechism adds the word *curse* to the concept of wrath. We need to understand the meaning of that word as it is used in Scripture. When our first parents sinned and fell in the garden, they came under the curse of death. In fact, this curse fell upon the whole of creation. Death became a principle, both for mankind and for all creation. When we think of the concept of the curse as a consequence of sin, we must go beyond just the temporal punishment that Adam and Eve suffered. The real curse associated with sin is everlasting separation from God. The Bible sometimes refers to this as death in the ultimate sense and sometimes as hell. Both words convey how dreadful sin is to God and for us.

The Larger Catechism has an interesting final word when it says, "and cannot be expiated except by the blood of Christ." There are two important truths in that expression. First of all, God has provided a way for us to escape His wrath and curse which sin deserves. Secondly, it tells us there is only one way this may be done. The blood of Christ cleanses us from all sin and saves us from the dreadful wrath and curse which we have brought upon ourselves because of our disobedience. The good news of the Gospel must always be understood and claimed in the light of this truth.

Question #85: *What doth God require of us, that we may escape his wrath and curse, due to us for sin?*

Answer: *To escape the wrath and curse of God, due to us for sin, God requireth of us faith in Jesus Christ, repentance unto life, with the diligent use of all the outward means whereby Christ communicateth to us the benefits of redemption.*

The bad news is every sin deserves the wrath and curse of God. The good news is God provides a way of escape. The catechism begins the study of salvation by asking, "What is required to escape the wrath and curse due to sin?" It is interesting that in a document in which the sovereignty of God and electing grace are the centerpieces of its theology, that a question like this could find a prominent place. For those who accuse Calvinists of ignoring or minimizing human responsibility, this question is a rebuke. The first requirement mentioned is faith in Christ. In a parallel passage in the Confession of Faith, the expression saving faith is justifying faith, and justifying faith is faith in Jesus Christ.

The faith spoken of here is faith that believes in the truth of the Gospel and faith that receives the Gospel. It is more than mere assent to propositional truth, though of course that is necessary. This kind of faith receives and rests upon Christ alone for salvation. Receiving implies commitment, and commitment speaks of relationship. So faith in Christ means we accept the truth God has revealed and we accept the Savior who meets us in the written Word.

The other requirement mentioned is repentance unto life. Repentance is called the missing doctrine in evangelical theology. However, it is only missing when evangelical theology is incomplete. It may be true many people minimize the need for repentance, but it is at the heart and soul of the Gospel we find in the Bible. The first public, recorded words of our Lord Jesus Christ are, *Repent and believe for the kingdom of heaven is at hand.* The whole ministry of John the Baptist was built around this central theme of repentance. The preaching of repentance has played a prominent role in every major revival since Pentecost. In fact, preaching of repentance was also prominent in the few incidences of national revival we find in the Old Testament.

Repentance involves several ingredients. First of all, there is an awareness of the holiness of God. That is the starting point for true repentance. It was Isaiah's vision of God and His holiness that led him to repentance. Repentance, however, not only looks upward to God, but inward to our hearts. When Isaiah saw God, he immediately became aware of his own sinful condition.

Repentance goes beyond awareness to confession. Confession is an open acknowledgment we have sinned and fallen short of the glory of God.

This, in turn, creates a spirit of sorrow: sorrow that we have offended God and that we failed to be all He has called us to be. This sorrow also includes a recognition of what we have missed by our sinfulness, but repentance is more than an attitude of regret and sorrow. Repentance is turning around from one direction and heading in another. A good example of this is the Apostle Paul. He started out for Damascus as Saul who hated Christ, but after meeting him on the road, his life was turned around and he went to Damascus to proclaim Christ. One final word, the catechism says that we must make diligent use of all outward means. That would imply the profitable use of every opportunity God affords for repentance and faith.

Question #86: *What is faith in Jesus Christ?*

Answer: *Faith in Jesus Christ is a saving grace, whereby we receive and rest upon him alone for salvation, as he is offered to us in the gospel.*

To understand the meaning of faith one must begin with another word, and that word is *grace*. The catechism refers to is at *saving grace*. In the book of Ephesians we read, *For be grace are ye saved through faith; and that not of yourselves: it is the gift of God: Not of works, lest any man should boast.* Faith is a gift. It comes to us by the grace of God.

Grace implies a gift unearned and undeserved. The grace of God reaches out to lost sinners with the most precious gift of all, the gift of faith. However, faith is a gift that must be received and exercised. Once we become the objects of grace, we are regenerated by the power of the Holy Spirit. This gives to us the ability and the responsibility to exercise faith in Jesus Christ. Mere faith, apart from Christ does not save us. Jesus Christ is our Savior and therefore faith must rest in Him. He is not only the author of our faith; He is the object of it as well. The catechism is very careful to weave the word *faith* into the word *grace* and the weaver is Jesus Christ.

This gift of faith enables us, according to the catechism, to do two things. First, we are enabled to receive Christ. In John 1:12 we read these words, *But as many as received him, to them gave he power to become the sons of God, even to them that believe on his name.* Receiving means more than merely believing, though it includes this. It also means that we accept the Lord Jesus as our personal savior. It means that we accept His gift from the cross. Receiving implies a relationship. We receive friends into our lives and into our hearts. The husband and the wife receive each other into a relationship of intimacy. Parents receive children into their lives. So in the catechism we are told that faith enables us to receive Christ and that receiving is very much like the above relationships.

The other word the catechism uses is the word *rest*. Faith enables us to rest upon Christ alone for salvation. This resting is basically trusting. To say that there is only one way of salvation in no way diminishes that one great way. He is the only savior, and He is the only one we will ever need. Resting upon Him only for salvation recognizes that great truth.

A final phrase in this statement, *as He is offered to us in the gospel*, is one that should be carefully considered and understood. Christ is offered to us in the Gospel in a particular way. We are not free to pick and choose, nor to suggest to God another way or another gospel. In the Gospel, He is presented to us as God the Son. One of the failures of many modern-day cults is the failure to recognize the full deity of Jesus Christ. Even though some very popular cults refer to him as the Son of God, they do not mean what the Bible means by that expression. Christ is God the Son, and in His own words, *I and the Father are one*. At the same time, we are told that He is also man, truly man. Furthermore, His saving work is that of a substitute. Christ died for our sins according to the Scripture. He was raised again from the dead and ascended into heaven. He will also come again to judge the living and the dead. In Isaiah 33:22 we read these words, *The Lord is our judge, the Lord is our lawgiver, the Lord is our King. He will save us*. This prophecy speaks of the Lord Jesus Christ, and this is what the catechism means when it says, *as He is offered to us in the gospel*. Believers are to make very, very sure of two things. One, that they have received the Lord Jesus Christ as He is offered in the Gospel; and two, we must be very sure that when we offer Him to other people, our offer is according to the Word of God.

Question #87: *What is repentance unto life?*

Answer: *Repentance unto life is a saving grace, whereby a sinner, out of a true sense of his sin, and apprehension of the mercy of God in Christ, doth, with grief and hatred of his sin, turn from it unto God, with full purpose of, and endeavor after, new obedience.*

"Faith and repentance are twin graces and they may be said to be born simultaneously. They may be separated in thought but not in experience; in logic but not in life. Faith of a kind precedes and produces repentance and faith of another kind follows and is the effect of repentance." So writes Dr. J.B. Green in his *Harmony of the Westminster Standards*. The catechism's answer to the question deals basically with the grounds and ingredients of repentance.

Let us first of all consider the grounds of repentance. The Shorter Catechism refers to repentance as saving grace. The Larger Catechism inserts these words, *wrought in the heart of a sinner by the spirit and word of God*. Right away we are given to understand that repentance is a product of regeneration. The unregenerate can never repent of sin in the true sense, nor can the regenerate ever live comfortably with it. Sovereign grace is the fountainhead of the graces we experience.

Humanly speaking, repentance springs out of two kinds of knowledge. First, there is the knowledge of the true sense of sin which is so basic to repentance. If we never see ourselves as sinners in the sight of God, we will never sense a need to repent. However, once we see ourselves through the eyes of God and see our sin as God sees it, then we are on the way to repentance. Jesus said, *Blessed are the poor in spirit: for theirs is the kingdom of heaven*. He also added, *Blessed are they that mourn: for they shall be comforted*. By these words our Lord described both the necessity and the essence of repentance. The one who is poor in spirit is the one who sees himself as a sinner in the sight of God. The one who mourns his condition will be comforted by the grace of forgiveness.

The other kind of knowledge involved in repentance is the knowledge of God's mercy in Christ. This comes about through understanding the Gospel. Paul wrote these incredible words concerning Christ: *He became sin for us who knew no sin that we might be made the righteousness of God in Him.* When we understand the mercy of God, then our repentance moves us into a saving relationship with the Lord Jesus Christ. However, we must remember it is all a work of God's sovereign grace and not of our own works.

The ingredients of repentance are likewise twofold. The first one is a grief and hatred for sin. When we realize that our sin offends God and was the cause of the death of our Lord Jesus Christ, then we can truly grieve over our sin. Too often our grief is superficial because it is grief over the consequences we must suffer. That is remorse, but not repentance. Our real grief over sin is the grief that we have caused God.

The second ingredient of repentance is turning from it unto God. Repentance is reversing our direction in thought as well as deed. Like faith, our repentance may be imperfect, but it may also be sincere. Repentance is not a just once-and-for-all experience; it is a daily turning to God. Unless the turning from sin involves a turning to God, with the full purpose of new obedience, then it will spend itself in emotion alone. There is emotion involved, but the emotion must prompt us to action or our repentance will be short-lived. Genuine repentance involves the whole man – his mind, his heart, and his will.

One final reminder is in order at this point. God alone can produce this kind of repentance in our lives.

Question #88: *What are the outward and ordinary means whereby Christ communicateth to us the benefits of redemption?*

Answer: *The outward and ordinary means whereby Christ communicateth to us the benefits of redemption are, his ordinances, especially the word, sacraments, and prayer; all of which are made effectual to the elect for salvation.*

This section of the catechism follows the treatment of repentance and faith. The catechism raises the question: What does God require of us to escape His wrath and curse because of sin? The answer is faith in Jesus Christ and repentance unto life. The same section of the catechism refers to a diligent use of all the outward means that Christ uses to communicate to us the benefits of His redemption.

Now the catechism deals with the question: what are these outward means? When the catechism uses the two words, *outward* and *ordinary*, it does not mean to say *insignificant* or *of little importance*. These words refer to the ways in which faith and repentance become living realities in the lives of believers.

Three of these outward means are mentioned – the word, sacraments, and prayer – and all of these are used by Christ to communicate to us the benefits of His redemption. The Word, of course, refers to our use of the Word of God and what it does in the life of the believer. In order for the Word to be operative in our lives, it must be read, understood, and applied. Later the catechism will emphasize the necessity of the Word being preached. Ordinarily, God calls the elect to Himself through the preaching of the Word. When the Word is read or heard in faith, there is a supernatural power at work in that process to draw us to God and to experience the actual working of His grace in our lives. It is therefore both dangerous and foolish for believers to neglect the Word.

Another expression the catechism uses is *the sacraments.* There are two: Baptism and the Lord's Supper. It is interesting to note that in the context of the times in which the catechism was written, the Westminster Divines did not allow the Roman Catholic misuse of the sacraments to distort their own view. Although they rejected the superstition associated with the sacraments, they recognized their value as a means of grace.

Baptism, being a sign and seal of the covenant, was given by the Lord and therefore becomes a means by which the truth of the Gospel becomes effective in our lives. The worth of this sacrament does not depend upon the one who administers it or even upon the one who receives it, but rather it derives its meaning from the God who gave it.

The Lord's Supper, the other sacrament recognized by Presbyterians, is a means of grace calling us to remember the atoning work of Christ. It reminds us of our relationship to Him and communicates the reality of His presence with His people.

The final expression is *prayer*. Although these three – the word, the sacraments, and prayer – are joined together, there is a special significance to the last of these. Prayer is a means of grace when the sinner prays for forgiveness and it is granted. Prayer continues to be a means of grace as the sinner confesses his sins and is assured that God is faithful and just to forgive us our sins and cleanse us from all unrighteousness. Prayer is a means of grace when we seek the guidance of the Holy Spirit in understanding the Word. Prayer is a means of grace when we intercede for fellow believers and pray for the coming of Christ's Kingdom. All three – the Word, sacraments, and prayer – are important in the lives of believers, and the neglect or misuse of them is a serious matter indeed. However, as we grow in the knowledge of the Word, our appreciation of the significance of the sacraments and our exercise of prayer, we experience the benefits of Christ's redemption.

Question #89: *How is the word made effectual to salvation?*

Answer: *The Spirit of God maketh the reading, but especially the preaching, of the word, an effectual means of convincing and converting sinners, and of building them up in holiness and comfort through faith unto salvation.*

The Bible is not just another book; it is the Word of God. Holy men of old spoke and wrote as they were moved by the Holy Spirit. These writings are literally God-breathed. This is what we mean when we say that the Bible is inspired.

The catechism asks: *How is the word made effectual to salvation?* The answer begins with the Holy Spirit. Even as the Spirit inspired the writing of the Word, so He must be active in the reading and hearing of the Word. His work is absolutely necessary to make the work of God effective in our lives. I have known many people who are well-read in the Bible and who have studied the Scriptures in depth and yet are not Christians. They can discuss and debate the finer points of the Scripture as if they were good theologians, but they have never been converted by those same Scriptures.

One aspect of the work of the Holy Spirit is to so illumine the Word and empower the Word as to regenerate the lost and edify the saints. The catechism puts special emphasis on the preaching of the Word as a means of converting sinners and edifying believers. Preaching by definition is expounding the Word of God. Anything less than this is simply not preaching in the Biblical sense. It may be informative and entertaining, but it is not preaching. In Biblical preaching, the style may vary, the application may be made by way of illustration, but at the heart of true preaching is the proclamation of God's Word. At its best, preaching is a supernatural event in which the living God meets with, and speaks His Word to, His people. This is not the work of man; it is the work of the Holy Spirit. The preacher's role is simply to be a servant of the Word and the Holy Spirit.

According to the catechism, the preaching of the Word has two major thrusts. One is convincing and converting of sinners. All too often this is overlooked in Presbyterian circles. However, the Bible always emphasizes the reaching of the lost through the preaching of the Word. Presbyterian preaching must include an effort to convince and convert sinners.

The other major theme of preaching is building up believers in holiness and bringing them comfort. One of the reasons why God converts sinners is to change them into His own image that He might have fellowship with them through all eternity. This requires that we grow in holiness, for in this we grow in likeness to our Father in heaven. The Scripture tells us to be holy, for the one who called us is holy. Holiness may be understood to be simply a reflection of the character of God. As children of God, His character grows in us through the word of the Holy Spirit and this comes about primarily through the preaching of the Word.

The catechism also uses the word *comfort*. Comfort should be always in the mind of God's messengers when the Word is preached, for our God is a God of all comfort. We in our own experience are surrounded constantly by pressure and sorrow, and this is the common lot of all mankind. The preacher who does not understand this and who fails in his ministry of comfort is not listening to the Holy Spirit, nor is he reflecting the heart of the God whom he represents.

In conclusion, the catechism uses two words, *faith* and *salvation*. The end and goal of all preaching is to produce faith that leads to salvation. When this is done, then the Spirit of God is making the Word of God effectual to salvation.

Question #90: *How is the word to be read and heard, that it may become effectual to salvation?*

Answer: *That the word may become effectual to salvation, we must attend thereunto with diligence, preparation, and prayer; receive it with faith and love, lay it up in our hearts, and practice it in our lives.*

A man once gave a friend a copy of the Bible. On the flyleaf he wrote four words which guided him in how to read it. These words were *admit, commit, submit,* and *transmit*. Whoever reads or hears the Bible with the view of doing these four things will find the reading and the hearing a blessed experience.

The way in which the Word is read or heard determines the

value of that reading or hearing. The reader or hearer's attitude toward the Bible is of fundamental importance. The Larger Catechism is an excellent commentary on the Shorter at this point. It teaches us that the Bible is to be read and heard with a desire to know, believe, and obey the will of God revealed therein. If one reads and hears with such a motive, then one will truly read with attention and diligence, with prayer and meditation, and will discover the truth the Bible teaches. But it is not enough that the Word would be read by all; it must be preached as well.

The catechism puts a high degree of importance on the preaching of the Word. The Larger Catechism develops this much more fully than the Shorter Catechism, and I encourage you to read and reflect on the Larger Catechism, questions 158 through 160. However, more can be said about the simple, straightforward statement which is found in the Shorter Catechism. We are told that there must be preparation and prayer in reading and hearing the Word. The kind of preparation that is necessary is that of prayer and a willing heart to understand and obey that Word.

We are also taught that it must be received with faith and love. Faith in the Word of God means believing that it is true and that it has authority in your life. Faith in the Word means that you trust the Bible in all that it says. This means believing that the Scriptures are God-breathed and, therefore, are beyond error or doubt.

Furthermore, we are to receive the Word with love. This speaks of an attitude of gratitude. We love God because He first loves us. We love His Word because through it we discover a personal relationship with God Himself. As the Psalmist says, *Oh how I love thy law O God, it is my mediation day and night*. In the long run you will discover that love for God and for His Word is the only enduring motivation to read and hear it. Although duty may make us diligent for a short while, only love will persevere and give us an eagerness of spirit that will allow nothing to replace the reading of God's Word.

The catechism teaches us that we are to lay it up in our hearts. Again we quote the Psalmist who said, *Thy Word have I hid in my heart that I might not sin against thee*. When Jesus said lay up for us treasures in heaven, He undoubtedly intended the laying up of God's

Word in our hearts as a part of this investment. Laying up God's Word in our hearts requires meditation and reflection. When I read or hear the Word of God, I must ask myself, what is God saying to me and how does this affect my life?

The final instruction in the catechism is that we are to practice it in our lives. Failure to do this will result in the loss of the knowledge that we might otherwise gain in the reading and hearing of the Word. So the catechism teaches us that those who read and hear the Word have a great responsibility and an even greater privilege.

Question #91: *How do the sacraments become effectual means of salvation?*

Answer: *The sacraments become effectual means of salvation, not from any virtue in them, or in him that doth administer them; but only by the blessing of Christ, and the working of his Spirit in them that by faith receive them.*

The place and importance of the sacraments in the Christian life has long been a subject of debate and division within the church. There are Christians who believe that the elements of the sacraments themselves are the means of grace, while other believers place little importance at all upon the sacraments.

Presbyterians have always tried to maintain a Biblical balance when it comes to the place and importance of the sacraments. We have already seen that the Bible as a means of grace must be heard in a certain way. The same thing is true of the sacraments. In order to receive the blessing of Christ through the sacraments, there must be a proper understanding of their meaning and importance. They must be that through which He bestows benefits and blessings upon us. The catechism makes it very plain that the blessing does not come through the ceremony of the sacrament or even through the one who administers them.

Sometimes Christians make the mistake of assuming that because the one who administers the sacrament is not a worthy servant of Christ, there is no virtue in the sacrament itself. I have talked to believers who wanted to be rebaptized because the one who administered baptism to them was not a true minister of Christ. This is to totally misunderstand the meaning of the sacraments. It is Christ who blesses the sacraments, not man. Therefore, baptism is received in the name of the triune God. The same thing is true of the Lord's Supper. Its virtue depends solely upon Christ working through it to produce repentance and faith in their lives.

The catechism goes on to point out that the work of the Holy Spirit is essential for the sacraments to become effectual means of salvation. The role of the Spirit is to interpret the meaning of the sacraments to those receiving them. It is through the baptism that we have been cleansed from sin by the blood of the everlasting covenant. In the Lord's Supper, He shows us that we are united to Christ both in His death and resurrection and that we are sustained by His grace.

Finally, the catechism points out the role of faith in the proper use of the sacraments. While it is true that the child of the covenant is incapable of exercising faith at the time of baptism, still the parents by faith look to the Lord Jesus for the salvation of their covenant child. Then as they are faithful in keeping their vows, the Holy Spirit works faith in the life of the covenant child in due time until that one comes to a saving faith in the Lord Jesus. Again, in the Lord's Supper we accept by faith the atonement that is demonstrated in the broken bread and the cup of the New Testament. We may go through the routine of the Lord's Supper a hundred times without the experience of even one blessing. When we come to the table in faith believing that Jesus died for us, then the sacrament becomes an effectual means of salvation in the life of the believer.

The Scripture tells us that without faith it is impossible to please God. It is also impossible to understand the work of grace illustrated by the sacraments unless they are received by faith.

Question #92: *What is a sacrament?*

Answer: *A sacrament is a holy ordinance instituted by Christ, wherein, by sensible signs, Christ and the benefits of the new covenant are represented, sealed, and applied to believers.*

When we were very young, we learned that a sacrament is an earthly sign with a heavenly meaning. That is fine so far as it goes, but it obviously does not go far enough. The Shorter Catechism gives a concise but for more complete definition, while the Larger Catechism and the Confession fill out the complete definition which we seek.

The first and most important thing which is taught in this statement from the catechism is that a sacrament is instituted by Christ Himself. This is what gives the sacraments their meaning and validity. It is not the prerogative of the church to institute sacraments, any more than it is her prerogative to claim her words are on par with Scripture, or that the deliverances of the church are new revelation beyond Scripture. It belongs to the church to proclaim the revelation already given, and to observe the sacraments already instituted.

The sacraments are called holy ordinances. This means they are actions and ceremonies which are God-ordained, and to be held in wonder and adoration because they depict the truths taught in God's Word. As Dr. Green once said, *The word is the gospel addressed to the ear, and the sacraments are the gospel addressed to the eye.*

When the catechism refers to the sacraments as sensible signs, it simply means they are signs or symbols which may be discerned at least in outward form by the physical senses. They may be seen, felt, and tasted. They would be meaningless without the Word, but as they are presented, in company with the Word, they accomplish God's purposes.

What are these purposes? There are several mentioned here, and more in the other documents of our standards. In these sensible signs Christ and the benefits of the new covenant are made known to believers.

First, Christ and these benefits are represented. That is to say, when we see the water of baptism, we are to understand that this represents cleansing. Water is the universal agent of washing or cleansing, and when the water of baptism is poured out upon believers and their infant seed, we are reminded of our need for cleansing, and God's grace in providing it. But there is far more than mere representation in this act. There is a sealing, a real act whereby the believer or the covenant child is sealed unto the day of redemption. Of course, this is not by the act alone, but rather by the grace of God working in and through the sign. Beyond sealing, there is also application of covenant blessings. What we have said of baptism is also true of the Lord's Supper. This is again a covenant act. It is a believer's feast. Since we are admonished in Scripture that we must discern the Lord's body, we first instruct our covenant children and admit them to the table upon their own profession of faith and examination by the session.

While it may be argued that some harm has been done and some of the splendor tarnished by too frequent observance of the Lord's Supper, it is equally true that we are spiritually impoverished by failure to observe the sacred meal more frequently than most of us do. Pastors and sessions would do well to study and pray fervently concerning this. Is the practice of very infrequent observance of the Lord's Supper really sufficient to encourage the saints in their walk with the Lord?

Question #93: *Which are the sacraments of the New Testament?*

Answer: *The sacraments of the New Testament are, baptism, and the Lord's supper.*

When the *Westminster Confession of Faith* and catechisms were written, the Reformed churches were in deep conflict with the Roman Catholic Church over the question of the sacraments. The Roman position was that the church had the authority to establish sacraments. Furthermore, the Church of Rome decreed that there were seven sacraments – baptism, the mass (the Lord's Supper), marriage, confirmation, penance, orders, and extreme unction. The Reformers held that there were only two sacraments as opposed to the seven of Rome. They came to this conclusion on the basis of the necessary tests to establish the nature of a sacrament.

First of all, it is required that a sacrament be instituted by the direct authority of Christ. Although the Lord gave approval of such things as marriage, there is never any indication that it was to be a means of grace to communicate salvation. Thus it could not possibly meet the requirement of direct institution by the Lord. So far as the other sacraments of the Roman church go, there is little, if any, Biblical ground for them, and certainly none suggesting that Christ directly instituted these things.

On the other hand, both baptism and the Lord's Supper came to us by direct commandment of the Lord to the disciples. In Matthew 28:19, we have one record of the command to baptize. This was part of the Great Commission and was to be administered in the name of the triune God.

The Lord's Supper was instituted by Christ in the Upper Room shortly before His arrest, trial, and death. Later, the Apostle Paul gave instruction concerning the Lord's Supper, saying, *I have received from the Lord that which I also delivered to you.* So it is obvious that these two sacraments meet that test of direct institution by the Lord.

The second test was that in the sacrament there must be an outward visible sign. Again, the additional five sacraments of the church of Rome do not all meet this test. It is obvious that the two sacraments accepted by the Reformers are built around the outward visible signs. In the case of baptism, the sign is water, and in the case of the Lord's Supper, bread and wine.

The third test has to do with the inward grace signified. The sacraments teach us by sensible sign the meaning of the saving and keeping grace of God. When this test is applied to the extra-Biblical sacraments instituted by the Church of Rome, again we find them failing to meet that Biblical standard. In the case of baptism and the Lord's Supper, their whole meaning is derived from the grace signified. In baptism, we signify the cleansing from sin. This cleansing is signified not only by the application of water as the universal agent of cleansing, but also as an illustration of the anointing of the Holy Spirit by which we are born again into the Kingdom of God.

The Lord's Supper signifies the death and resurrection of our Lord. The bread and cup signify the body broken and the blood shed, but since Jesus added the promise that He would eat this meal again in the Kingdom of God, we also understand it speaks of the resurrection. Further, it signifies our enduring communion with the Lord. Just as we receive the bread and the fruit of the vine physically, so we receive Christ spiritually by faith and are nurtured by His abiding presence. So the sacraments of the New Testament are two only – the Lord's Supper and baptism. These alone fulfill the requirements for a true sacrament.

Question #94: *What is baptism?*

Answer: *Baptism is a sacrament, wherein the washing with water, in the name of the Father, and of the Son, and of the Holy Ghost, doth signify and seal our ingrafting into Christ, and partaking of the benefits of the covenant of grace, and our engagement to be the Lord's.*

As we start to explore the meaning of the sacraments beginning with baptism, we see how thoroughly consistent the catechism is with the teaching of Scripture. Baptism is a sacrament which has been instituted by Christ not only as a sign, but also as a seal of the benefits of the new covenant to believers.

The catechism begins by describing baptism in these words, *the washing with water in the name of the Father, the Son, and the Holy Ghost.* Although the mode of baptism is not dealt with in the catechism, it is worth a moment of our time to consider this a bit further. In both sacraments of the New Testament there is representation of a reality that is greater than that which we see on the surface. Just as the blood of bulls and goats could not atone for sin, so the actual practice of baptism cannot wash the soul and make it clean. Therefore, it is proper to symbolize this washing in a way that is appropriate for all believers and their children under any circumstance.

Baptism by sprinkling or pouring is clearly supported by Biblical descriptions in both the Old and New Testaments. Two brief examples will serve to illustrate this. In the tabernacle, the altar and the various implements of worship were ceremonially cleansed by the sprinkling of blood and water. It is not to be imagined that such a ceremony actually cleansed either the altar or the other furnishings of the tabernacle. Rather, this was a symbolic representation that God had purified the tabernacle for His own use. In the New Testament, the baptism of the Apostle Paul is one of the most significant events recorded. The command to Paul was to arise and be baptized and his response was immediate. The Bible says he arose and was baptized. There is no indication he left the location to accompany Ananias to a pool or river. He simply arose and was baptized on the spot.

However, the real significance of baptism has little to do with the mode or method. It is obvious the mode was not the major preoccupation of the Westminster scholars, since the Shorter Catechism does not speak to this at all. Their intent was to explain what is symbolized by the act of baptism.

Three things are signified by baptism as explained in the Shorter Catechism. First of all, there is our ingrafting into Christ. This simply means that baptism is to show that we have not only identified with Christ, but have become part of His body on earth, the Church. The second thing signified by baptism is that we are partaking the benefits of the covenant of grace. These benefits are several: justification, adoption, regeneration, sanctification, and finally glorification. So baptism anticipates things that will take place in the life of believers as well as the gracious acts of God on their behalf. Finally, the catechism refers to *our engagement to be the Lord's*. That expression is meant to convey that baptism is a public announcement of our relationship with Christ. In this ceremony, we publicly and willingly commit ourselves to Christ and to His Kingdom, and by this outward sign we bear testimony to the inward grace which has taken place in our lives.

The catechism also refers to baptism as more than just a sign; it is also a seal. This means that beyond the outward ceremony of baptism, there is real grace imparted to and experienced by the believer.

Question #95: *To whom is baptism to be administered?*

Answer: *Baptism is not to be administered to any that are out of the visible church, till they profess their faith in Christ, and obedience to him; but the infants of such as are members of the visible church, are to be baptized.*

It sounds like an innocent enough question, but the answers have been causes of fundamental division within the Christian church. Before the Reformation, infant baptism was seldom if ever questioned. It was historical fact from the days of the Apostles that believers and their infant seed were baptized into the church. However, in the development of the Reformation, there arose a sect known as the Anabaptists that maintained only believers were to be baptized and then (among many of them) only by immersion. This was an extreme reaction to the abuses of baptism that existed in the medieval church.

The catechism in answering this question speaks to the issue of the objects of baptism and also the meaning of baptism. We believe it is also proper for the children of believing parents to be baptized.

In the Presbyterian Church we do not baptize all children, but only the children of Christian parents. A child is accepted for baptism if only one parent is a professing Christian.

Probably every Presbyterian minister has been asked at one time or another, "Will you *christen* our baby next Sunday?" We do not Christen children in the church, for that is the rite by which a name is given. We do not confer a name upon a child, but by the name given to the child by the parents we baptize the child.

What is the meaning of baptism, especially as it applies to the baptism of infants? First of all, we acknowledge that they are a part of the body of Christ on earth. We refer to our baptized children as noncommuning members. This means they are not entitled to all of the privileges of church membership, but they are acknowledged to be part of the family. When they come of age, they must make their own profession of faith, and at that time will be received into the church as full members with all the privileges and rights of membership.

One illustration of this is seen when a child born of American parents in a foreign country comes under the protection of the United States government. Until the age of 18, that child is regarded as a citizen by birth, but if he wishes to retain that membership, he must sign papers confirming his citizenship before he can vote, and he must also take a vow of allegiance to the United States. This is an excellent illustration of a child's membership in the body of Christ. That child is to be regarded as being a member under the protection and care of the church, but when he comes of age, he must make his own profession of faith and take his vows of membership.

Secondly, the baptism of infants is a sign and seal of the covenant of grace. When we present our children for baptism, we claim for them the benefits of the covenant and the blessings which God has promised to believers and their children. The most important of these is found in these words, *I will be a God unto you and unto your children after you throughout all generations.*

Finally, we baptize our children as a sign of our own dedication to their upbringing in the Lord. The outward sign then is not only upon the child, but upon the parents who make promises to God on behalf of their children. In this ceremony the parents acknowledge that their child belongs to God and that it is their responsibility to teach their child the truths of the Christian faith. One of the most glorious privileges and solemn responsibilities Christian parents have is to claim the benefits of the covenant for their children as well as themselves.

Question #96:   *What is the Lord's supper?*

Answer: *The Lord's supper is a sacrament, wherein, by giving and receiving bread and wine, according to Christ's appointment, his death is showed forth; and the worthy receivers are, not after a corporal and carnal manner, but by faith, made partakers of his body and blood, with all his benefits, to their spiritual nourishment and growth in grace.*

When the catechism explains the meaning of the Lord's Supper, it begins by mentioning the elements involved. According to the catechism, bread and wine are given and received. There is an ongoing debate in Christian circles as to the exact nature of the substance of the cup. Nowhere in Scripture is this clearly stated. Ordinarily the expression *the cup* is all that is used. The only other words were the words of Jesus when He referred to the fruit of the vine.

Probably more has been made than is wise or necessary over this matter. However, a word of caution is in order for those who insist on the use of wine. People who have had a problem with alcoholism in the past have mentioned to me on several occasions that both the taste and the odor of the wine has been a real stumbling block for them in the observance of the Lord's Supper. This should cause us to be very careful lest in the observance of the Lord's Supper, occasion be given for unnecessary temptation to be placed before a weaker brother.

The catechism in explaining the meaning of the elements mentions two basic truths. First, that the giving of the bread and the wine are a showing forth the death of Christ. Presbyterians have always rejected the doctrines of transubstantiation and consubstantiation as being unbiblical. While we believe that the elements themselves simply represent the body and blood of Christ, we believe that it is a true representation, and although Christ is not present in the physical sense, He is most surely present in a spiritual sense. Therefore, when we feed physically upon the elements, we are feeding spiritually upon the reality of Christ and His atonement. Furthermore, the catechism tells us that we are made partakers by faith of His body and blood and all His benefits. To partake of the body and blood of Christ is to have a part in His body, the Church, and to be in the family of God. The Apostle Paul goes on to say that we are heirs of God and joint heirs with Christ. When we think of the benefits that Christ gave to His people, we think in terms of forgiveness and justification. In this way the Lord's Supper becomes a means of grace to communicate to us the blessings of salvation.

The expressions *spiritual nourishment* and *growth in grace* naturally go together. When the child is nourished physically, that child grows physically as well. When believers are spiritually nourished, they also grow in grace and in likeness to Christ. So the Lord's Supper then becomes one of the ways in which we grow as believers.

It is sad but true that Protestants in general, and Presbyterians in particular, have tended to minimize the importance of the Lord's Supper, and thus have denied themselves one form of spiritual nourishment and the growth that results from it. When the elders in Geneva denied John Calvin's request to include the Lord's Supper in every worship service and limited its observance to four times a year, they set a pattern for Presbyterians that has been to our detriment. When we properly prepare ourselves and instruct our people in the true meaning of the word *supper*, then a more frequent observance of this sacrament would seem to be in order.

Question #97: *What is required to the worthy receiving of the Lord's supper?*

Answer: *It is required of them that would worthily partake of the Lord's supper, that they examine themselves, of their knowledge to discern the Lord's body, of their faith to feed upon him, of their repentance, love, and new obedience; lest coming unworthily, they eat and drink judgement to themselves.*

Who is worthy to come to the Lord's table? The answer is simple: No one is worthy. Who may come to the Lord's table in a worthy manner? All believers may partake in a worthy manner, but not all do so.

The question of worthiness to partake of the Lord's Supper has been a thorny issue and a matter of debate from the beginning of the Christian church. There have been (predictably) two extremes on the question and, like most extremes, both are wrong.

Some err on the side of having no restrictions placed on the Lord's table. In some churches there is never a word of warning, exhortation, or even explanation for those who come to the Lord's table.

On the other hand, there are those who, in their zeal to "fence the table," make it all but impossible for any save a select few believers to partake of the Lord's Supper. In the early days of my own ministry, I served a congregation of people who had been taught that no one should come to the Lord's table unless they were totally free from sin. So on a given Communion Sabbath, out of a congregation of well over one hundred, no more than a half-dozen or so would ever partake of the Lord's Supper.

The Apostle Paul dealt with this whole question when he wrote to the church in Corinth. He warned against a frivolous observance of the Lord's Supper and instructed all those who would participate to examine themselves. You will note that Paul did not tell believers to examine each other, but rather to examine their own hearts. There has been a tendency in Presbyterian circles to reverse that priority. I am not saying it is improper for sessions to exercise spiritual leadership or even discipline, but *self*-examination is the primary requisite in preparation for the Lord's Supper.

The catechism emphasizes this when we are exhorted to examine ourselves as to knowledge, faith, repentance, love, and obedience. The knowledge that we are instructed to have is the knowledge that enables us to understand what we do when we come to the table and what the elements signify. This is one reason why traditionally Presbyterians have required covenant children to be trained and examined by the session before they are admitted to the Lord's table. In some circles of Presbyterianism, this time-honored practice is being abandoned and even the smallest of children, who understand little if anything about the meaning of the Lord's Supper, are allowed to participate. This would seem to violate both our own standards and the clear teaching of Scripture.

Another requirement is that of repentance. When we examine ourselves in light of God's Word, the most obvious thing is that we are all sinful people and need forgiveness. Repentance means that we acknowledge this and seek God's grace and power to overcome the sin in our lives.

We are also required to renew our love, faith, and obedience. None of us love the Lord as we should, nor is our faith as strong as it ought to be. However, the Lord's Supper affords a wonderful time to pledge again our love to Christ, to renew our faith, and to determine the practice of more faithful obedience. It is interesting to note the Larger Catechism encourages weak, doubting Christians to come to the Lord's table in order that their faith might be strengthened, and their doubt resolved. If we did more to encourage this, we might find our people blessed and strengthened by participation in the Lord's Supper, rather than being discouraged by their insufficiencies.

Question #98: *What is prayer?*

Answer: *Prayer is an offering up of our desires unto God, for things agreeable to his will, in the name of Christ, with confession of our sins, and thankful acknowledgment of his mercies.*

The three means of grace mentioned in the catechism are the Word, the sacraments, and prayer. We come now to the last of these – prayer.

In the Shorter Catechism we have an answer to the question: *What is prayer?* This shows the Shorter Catechism at its finest. The answer to this ninety-eighth question ranks in quality with the magnificent first question and answer.

The practice of prayer requires an understanding of its essential nature and that's what makes this statement from the catechism so important. Here we have precise instructions on the nature of prayer, the manner of prayer, and the content of prayer.

First of all, the catechism acknowledges the reality of our communication with God through prayer. Because prayer is an offering up of our desires unto God, this implies both an emotional and knowledgeable exercise. Prayer must never be offered to any save God alone. As Protestants and Presbyterians, we reject the concept of praying to the saints. However, upon closer examination, we will discover that many of our public prayers are precisely that. Far too often we are more aware of those with whom we pray than Him to whom we pray. While we should pray for the benefit of others who hear our prayers, we must never fall into the trap of praying to be heard and seen by them. The perfect model of public prayer is the high priestly prayer of our Lord. There in the presence of His disciples, the Lord Jesus lifted up His eyes and heart to heaven and prayed to the Father. Every word He spoke was addressed directly to the Father, and every word was a blessing and encouragement to His disciples.

When we bring our desires before the Lord, we are to do so openly and sincerely. At the same time, these desires must be tempered by two important considerations: the will of God and the name of Christ. These two considerations are closely entwined. To pray for things according to the will of God is to pray for those things for which Jesus taught us to pray. Why is it so important to pray in the name of Christ? The answer is twofold. Christ is the sinless and perfect and only mediator between God and man, while we are sinful and cannot enter the presence of the holy God apart from Christ's righteousness and intercession.

The content of all our prayers may be summed up in three phrases: *Offering up of our desires*; *Confession of our sins*; and *Thankful acknowledgment of his mercies*. It is so very important that we not allow the confession of sin and the offering up of our desires to consume all of our time in prayer. Of course, these things are important, but not so important that we can afford to ignore the thankful acknowledgment of God's mercies. This means that much of our time in prayer should be spent in praise and adoration. We should thank Him for His mighty works of creation and redemption, and, as we seek His blessing, we should also thank Him without ceasing for the blessings already received. If we really understand and practice what the catechism teaches about prayer, we will discover a greatly enriched prayer life and a closeness to the Lord which we have not known before.

Question #99: *What rule hath God given for our direction in prayer?*

Answer: *The whole word of God is of use to direct us in prayer; but the special rule of direction is that form of prayer, which Christ taught his disciples, commonly called, "The Lord's prayer."*

The catechism mentions prayer as a means of grace. While it may not be technically correct to regard prayer as a means of grace, it is certainly a most essential part of worship. It is also undeniably an avenue of great blessing.

When the question is asked, *what rule has God given us for our direction in prayer,* it is interesting to note that the Larger Catechism refers to prayer as a duty, while the Shorter Catechism does not use the word, though it supports the Larger in the concept that prayer is a duty as well as a privilege. As someone has said, a prayerless person is essentially a Godless person.

However, unless our prayers are guided by the Word of God and aided by the Spirit of God, they may go far astray from the will of God. There is a tendency in some evangelical circles to use prayer as a demand on God. It is not too rare to hear people say, "In the name of Jesus, I demand that this person be healed," or a similar statement. Such prayer is not Biblical and insults God's sovereignty.

Our catechism says the whole Word of God is to be used as a primer on prayer. To be able to pray according to Scripture requires us to know Scripture, especially those parts of Scripture that deal with prayer. We find the prayers of God's people recorded in the Word from the very beginning to the end. One of the more profitable ways to learn to pray is to study these prayers and to learn to pray as men of old. Daniel's prayers are outstanding examples of effective prayer. Many Psalms are prayers and it is appropriate to adopt the language and spirit found in the Psalms.

The catechism, however, points us in particular to the Lord's Prayer as our model. Again, the Larger Catechism addresses the question of how the Lord's Prayer is to be used. It points to the Lord's Prayer as a pattern, but also as a prayer that may be offered by believers. Our primary concern in the study of the Lord's Prayer will be to learn how it may be used as a pattern for all our praying.

In the Lord's Prayer, we discover that prayer is to be addressed to God, and to God as our Father. The Lord's Prayer is the prayer, therefore, of children. There is an exclusiveness about the Lord's Prayer because not everyone may properly address God as heavenly Father. This is a right reserved for believers in Jesus Christ and for them alone. So the beginning point of prayer is to make sure of the proper relationship with God that affords us a hearing. While it may be true that in the general sense God hears the prayers of all people, this is true only in a very general sense. Certainly God is aware of all prayers, for He is all-knowing. But true communication and fellowship come only through our Lord Jesus Christ. Some people object to the use of the Lord's Prayer in corporate worship on the grounds that not everyone who attends church is necessarily a believer. It seems to me that this is unnecessarily judgmental. God knows those who are His and accepts their prayers as a Father hearing his children. The church is the body of Christ on earth; and, therefore, it is proper for the church to address the Father in the language which was taught us by our Lord Jesus Christ.

For Christians, it is not enough just to say the words of the Lord's Prayer, but to be taught the art of prayer by its form, its content, and its spirit. These things we will explore further in our study.

Question #100: *What doth the preface of the Lord's prayer teach us?*

Answer: *The preface of the Lord's prayer, which is, "Our Father which art in heaven," teacheth us to draw near to God, with all holy reverence and confidence, as children to a father, able and ready to help us; and that we should pray with and for others.*

The Lord's Prayer is an answer to prayer. It was given at the request of Jesus' disciples who said, *Lord, teach us to pray*. This is how Jesus taught His disciples and us to pray. If we follow His formula for prayer and understand its meaning, we will truly know how to pray. If we know how to pray, we will know God. He will bless us. All the infinite resources of heaven will be placed at our disposal. Our faith will increase, and we will develop a warm and personal relationship with the living God.

The preface to the Lord's Prayer teaches us that we may address God as our Father; however, this is not an open invitation to people apart from Christ. We must remember that Jesus taught His disciples to pray in this manner. He was the one who said, *No man comes to the Father but by Me*. The privilege of calling God our Father is a gift from Jesus Christ to those who love and trust Him as their Savior.

Christ made it very clear in His teaching that not everyone can call God Father. He even said to those who opposed Him, *You are of your father, the devil*. He constantly reminded His disciples that there is coming a day of final separation, which will divide people for all time. Some will go to be with their Father in heaven, and others will be expelled from His presence. So as soon as we begin to pray, *Our Father*, we are to pause and ask, *Is He my Father? Have I claimed His Son as my Savior so that I may call Him Father?*

Once this issue is settled and we know that we belong to Jesus Christ, then we may truly call God our Father and know that He loves and cares for us. We may be assured that He is more eager to bless us than we are to receive the blessing. We may know that our sins have been forgiven and that we have a Father and a home.

When we pray, *Our Father*, we do not stop there but go on to say, *who art in heaven*. This adds a dimension to our prayer life that is sorely missing in many prayers. Yes, we may have an intimate, personal relationship with God, and we may call Him our Father; but He is also the almighty, the ever-living God of eternity, sovereign in all His ways. He is the great and able God to whom we come when we pray, *Our Father who art in heaven*. He is able to do far more abundantly than we are able to ask or think. He has a perfect will and the power to perform it. He knows just what answer to your prayer is best for you and will accomplish His will in your life. When you pray, you pray to a holy, almighty, and powerful God, who in Jesus Christ has become your Father in heaven.

This Father loves you. He knows you, and both His knowledge and His love are perfect. Your every need is known before you request His help. Every tear that falls from your eye is felt by Him. He hears every weary sigh, every inward groan. He desires to heal you. He waits for you with eager arms of love and acceptance. He has given you His Son; will He not also freely give you all things?

When you pray, be still and know that He is God. Before you confess a single sin, before you ask one blessing for yourself or another, call upon your Father in heaven. Be aware that you are in His presence, rejoice in Him, and be glad.

When you pray, say, *Our Father who art in heaven.*

Question #101: *What do we pray for in the first petition?*

Answer: *In the first petition, which is, "Hallowed by thy name," we pray, that God would enable us, and others, to glorify him in all that whereby he maketh himself known, and that he would dispose all things to his own glory.*

One of the great lessons of the Lord's Prayer is to be found in its order. In this prayer, first things come first, and each part logically follows the other. There is the beauty of symmetry in this prayer, and the even greater beauty of truth.

The first petition focuses not upon the need of the one who prays, but on the God to whom we pray. This is always a must in true prayer. If our attention is not focused upon the Lord, our prayers are little more than wishes spoken aloud. But if we are aware of the great God before whom we come, then prayer is a reality of communication and relationship with the Most High. So when you pray, think first of God, your heavenly Father.

I think it would be clear to all the readers of this book that this prayer is truly for children only, and we are only children of the Father by faith in His Son, the Lord Jesus Christ. For children, the Father Himself is our first concern in prayer. Our desire is to know Him and to glorify Him. This petition expresses that desire. By these words we are asking that we, and indeed all people, might truly know God through His own self-revelation; and that knowing Him, we might also honor and glorify Him.

In the Bible we meet the one true God who is Creator and Savior. He is sovereign, gracious, and holy. He is the one who said, *Let be*, and the universe came into existence. Yet He is also the Good Shepherd who tenderly cares for His sheep and seeks out those who have gone astray to return them to the fold again. He is the God of the covenant who works all things together for good to those who love Him, to those who are called according to His purpose. So when we pray, *Hallowed be thy name*, we are asking that we may know Him as He thus reveals Himself. The psalmist sings, *O magnify the Lord with me, and let us exalt his name together.* We do not, and indeed, cannot, add to the glory and greatness of His name, but we may, and must, ascribe to Him that greatness and glory. We are commanded to proclaim His name and wonders throughout the whole earth. Furthermore, we who are called by the name of His Son (Christians) pray that our lives may indeed honor that great name.

Lack of reverence for God's name is one of the most terrible sins of this generation. Be warned! God will not hold him guiltless who takes His name in vain. Profanity and blasphemy are so common that some people never hear the name of our God save when it is taken in vain. What a tragedy! We pray that the name of God may be reverenced, for the name of God reveals the character of God.

All other petitions flow from this one. Whatever requests we may bring before the Lord must be ones that honor Him and that great name by which we make our requests known.

This is a petition of great hope and promise. For when we pray, *Hallowed be thy name*, we are reminded that the day will come when every knee shall bow and every tongue confess that Christ is Lord, to the glory of God the Father.

———

Question #102: *What do we pray for in the second petition?*

Answer: *In the second petition, which is, "Thy kingdom come," we pray, that Satan's kingdom may be destroyed, and that the kingdom of grace may be advanced, ourselves and others brought into it, and kept in it, and that the kingdom of glory may be hastened.*

One of the universal dreams of all people everywhere has been the dream of a golden age. Some look back to the good old days of long ago – but they were never really that good. Others speak of a coming age of peace and perfection. All through the ages people have written about an ideal kingdom, a hidden Utopia.

There is a reality behind these dreams. It is the kingdom of God. This kingdom was foretold by the prophets and proclaimed by Christ and His apostles. In its completed form, it is truly the fulfillment of this age-long dream. It will be a kingdom of righteousness, of peace, of fulfillment, and perfection.

In these words which Christ taught His disciples to pray, the hopes and dreams of mankind become the prayer of the believer: *Thy kingdom come.* Notice again the logical order of this prayer. We began by addressing the great God of heaven as our Father. We adore and worship Him and pray that His name might be honored. Immediately following this we pray, *Thy kingdom come.*

The theme of much of Christ's preaching and teaching was the kingdom of God. His first public proclamation was "Repent and believe, for the Kingdom of heaven is at hand." Most of His parables had to do with the kingdom. One of His last recorded acts on earth was to receive a dying thief into His kingdom.

But what is the kingdom of God? In what sense do we pray for its coming? The simplest answer is that the kingdom of God is the rule of God in the lives of people. This may be expanded to include factors such as extent, time, and nature; but basically the kingdom of God is a relationship between God and man.

To pray, *Thy kingdom come,* is a prayer for things in the

present tense. We pray for God to extend His kingdom into the hearts and minds of people everywhere. Thus, this is a missionary prayer. It should ever be in the heart and on the lips of every believer. We cannot bring the kingdom in ourselves, but we can pray that God will cause His kingdom to come.

John Calvin posed the question, *In what sense do we pray 'thy kingdom come'?* His answer reads, *That day by day the Lord may increase the number of faithful, that day by day He may increasingly bestow His graces upon them until He has fulfilled them completely.* By this prayer, we pray for the success of the Gospel and the conversion of the lost.

At the present time, the kingdom of God is in conflict with the powers of darkness and sin. Satan and sin rule the heart of natural man. Paul referred to Satan as being *the god of this world*, so the kingdom of God and the kingdom of Satan are at war when we pray, *Thy kingdom come*. We are aware of this conflict and pray for the overthrow of evil. As Christians, we have an obligation to join sides in this war. Neutrality is impossible.

This can be a dangerous prayer for you. Do you really want the overthrow of evil within your own heart? Do you really want to give up your pride and greed, your evil thoughts and hasty tongue? To pray *Thy kingdom come* in a personal way may lead to change, upheaval, and disruption in your life. You must be prepared to face the consequences of this prayer.

Finally, this prayer has a future dimension. Peter said we are looking for a hastening to the coming of the day of the Lord. So we are praying for the return of Christ and the ushering in of the kingdom in all of its glory and wonder.

Question #103: *What do we pray for in the third petition?*

Answer: *In the third petition, which is, "Thy will be done in earth as it is in heaven," we pray, that God, by his grace, would make us able and willing to know, obey, and submit to his will in all things as the angels do in heaven.*

When one of the great Puritan ministers lay dying, his last words were, *Lord, what you will, where you will, and how you will.* In these words, he was expressing not only his faith, but a summary of his entire life. He had lived to do the will of God and was happy to die in the will of God.

When we pray, *Thy will be done*, we are praying a prayer that will always be answered. God is sovereign; He rules and overrules in all things and in all places. In the drama of human history, He is the leading actor and all people no matter how great or small play a supporting role to Him.

There is, however, another sense in which this prayer is not being answered yet. There is so much in the world that opposes God and is contrary to His will. There is so much hatred, so many wars, so much violence, so much infidelity to truth, so much pollution of the mind, so much abuse of the weak and the helpless. No, we cannot say God's will is being done on earth as it is in heaven.

In this petition, we find an affirmation of faith. This is our firm belief, our cherished conviction, our life experience with God. We believe in God's authority and power, and we deny that either chance or evil is in control. We believe the providence of God is actively at work. Though evil may seem to be in control, in the final sense we can never accept this illusion.

God is Lord. This is the only life-view that makes sense or can deliver us from despair. The Christian believes every joy or sorrow, every victory or defeat is part of the often-mysterious but always-loving plan and purpose of God. This does not mean we surrender to apathy or evil, but rather that in the end God will triumph. We may not always be able to explain the events of the moment or how they fit into God's loving purpose, but we do believe that God is in control and ultimately His will will be done.

This prayer is more than just an affirmation of faith – it is an act of commitment. When we pray, *Thy will be done*, we are engaging in a personal act of dedication and commitment which has great significance in our own lives. We are saying in effect that we want to know God's will and pledge ourselves to do it. This will mean a surrender of self and a forsaking of sin. This will also mean a readjusting of priorities. When I pray, *Thy will be done*, I must mean "in me." The idea is to present our bodies as living sacrifices unto God, holy and acceptable, which is our reasonable service. Martin Luther once prayed, *Oh Father, do not let me fall so low as to insist that my will be done. Break my will, put obstacles in my way, that come what may, not my will, but Thine be done.*

It is easy to say these words. It is much more difficult to sincerely mean them. Our example is that of the Lord Jesus Christ in the Garden of Gethsemane when He gave His will over to the will of the Father.

Finally, this prayer is an ideal for which we long. The petition is not complete until we add, *in earth as it is in heaven.* By these words, we look in faith for the sure and certain future. This petition contains an eternal dimension. Although it points to a future age, it has bearing on the present age in which we live. We pray for the perfections of heaven to be at work in our lives even now. God has promised a new heaven and a new earth wherein dwells righteousness. When we pray this prayer, we claim that promise and commit ourselves to that ideal.

Question #104: *What do we pray for in the fourth petition?*

Answer: *In the fourth petition, which is, "Give us this day our daily bread," we pray, that, of God's free gift, we may receive a competent portion of the good things of this life, and enjoy his blessing with them.*

In the Lord's Prayer, there is an abrupt transition from the lofty things of God and His Kingdom down to the everyday need of people. One might expect the Lord to deal first with the needs of the spirit, with forgiveness and cleansing, but this is not the case.

The Lord was being perfectly logical and consistent. After all, the spirit resides within a human body. That body must be fed and its needs met. There could be no piety or dedication without food. There could be no act of worship, no self-denying piety, no winning souls for Christ unless the body is maintained.

There are other petitions immediately following this one which remind us, *man does not live by bread alone*. However, in this petition attention is turned toward the physical and material needs which God has promised to provide. This fourth petition is the practical consequence of the first three. Only one who calls upon God as his father, seeks God's glory and kingdom, and prays for the will of God to be accomplished in his own life can pray with expectation, *give us this day our daily bread*. This petition recognizes the goodness of God.

The eternal God, Creator of the universe, knows and cares about your every need. The hairs of your head are numbered. The thoughts of your mind are known. Isaiah says all nations are but a drop in the bucket before God. But the same Bible tells us not even a sparrow falls to the ground without your heavenly Father. God provides and cares. Therefore, you may call upon Him for your own personal needs with the same confidence by which you pray, *thy kingdom come*. There are other passages in the Bible which teach that it is proper for us to call on God for our physical needs. With the right attitude and purpose, we may pray for God to bless us materially if we are willing to accept the fact that He may chose not to do so. God knows our every need, and in His wisdom and sovereignty He will supply whatever is best for us. We must also remember that the Bible constantly warns against allowing material things to be of utmost importance. It is easy to come under bondage to things. Jesus said, *Seek first the kingdom of God and His righteousness and all these things will be added unto you.*

This petition recognizes our dependence upon God. There are no other words in the Bible which express so fully and completely our utter dependence upon God. Even though we may be prosperous and secure at any given moment, yet our daily bread is a gift form God. You may be perfectly sound of mind and body with a secure position of loving family and respect of fellow man, but all of these things may vanish in a moment without warning. We tend to forget in our complex technological society that our daily bread still comes from the simple processes of nature. Our dependence upon God is day by day and moment by moment. When Israel was in the wilderness, they were given just enough manna for that day and no more. What a tremendous parable this is for our lives. God intends us to trust Him on a daily basis and not to gather to ourselves the imagined security of wealth and possession. These things are not wrong in themselves, but trusting them instead of God is a deadly sin.

One final word of reminder is in order. This prayer is in the plural. It must never be prayed as a selfish prayer. Jesus did not say, *give me this day my daily bread,* but *give us this day our daily bread.*

Question #105: *What do we pray for in the fifth petition?*

Answer: *In the fifth petition, which is, "And forgive us our debts, as we forgive our debtors," we pray, that God, for Christ's sake, would freely pardon all our sins; which we are the rather encouraged to ask, because by his grace we are enabled from the heart to forgive others.*

When we pray, *forgive us our debt, as we forgive our debtors*, we are touching the heart and soul of Christian doctrine and Christian life. This petition helps us to clearly see that the Lord's Prayer is a prayer for the children of God exclusively. Only the merits of Christ's righteousness and the shedding of His blood can win for us the right to ask for forgiveness, and only the person in whom the living Christ lives can offer forgiveness to others.

Years ago I heard a story that has impressed this petition on my mind. It was the story of a tombstone in a neglected old churchyard. There was no name or date on the tombstone. There was but one word, "Forgiven." Truly, this tells the story of every Christian, and this is the only epitaph that really counts.

This petition is filled with the message of the Gospel and proclaims the atonement. It focuses on the cross and what our Lord did there. Our greatest need is the need for forgiveness. Apart from this, we are truly lost souls without God and without hope. The good news of the Gospel meets this greatest need.

There is a sense in which this is a once-and-for-all prayer. There must come a time in one's life when one comes to grips with the problem of sin. The circumstances may vary but the need is the same. We may come before God as the publican in the Temple, oppressed and overborne with such guilt that we can only cry out, "God have mercy on me the sinner." Or we may come as the rich young ruler, knowing something is missing and having no peace. Again, we may be as Nicodemus, coming furtively, yet with a real hunger and need for relief. But sooner or later we must pray this prayer or we can never see the kingdom of God.

One the other hand, this is more than just a once-and-for-all prayer. We must pray this prayer every day and every hour in the day. The promise of the Word to believers is if we confess our sins, God is faithful and just to forgive us our sins and to cleanse us from all unrighteousness. When we come before God in prayer, we must always be aware of our need to confess sin and receive forgiveness.

In this petition, we confess our evil thoughts, our cruel and careless words, our every betrayal of confidence and trust, our every denial of faith. We confess our selfish motives and outlook, the deeds that displease God and hurt our fellow man. This petition also requires us to confess our sins of omission and failure. We ask forgiveness for not being kind, for not being concerned. We ask God to forgive us for not loving each other and bearing each other's burdens.

When we pray, *Forgive us our debts*, we must follow along with the words, *as we forgive our debtors*. This is the only petition the Lord took time to explain and underscore by way of illustration. If you have been forgiven by God, you must forgive. You cannot help yourself or even want to. If Christ is living in you, your heart will not be cold, hard, and unforgiving. Of course, it costs to forgive other people, but it cost God far more to forgive you than it ever cost you to forgive your brother. It cost the Lord Jesus His life; and the Father, His precious Son.

What are we to forgive? Anything and everything. How often or how much? As often as the need is there. Jesus' words to Simon Peter were *seventy times seven*, which simply means there must be an inexhaustible supply of forgiveness within your heart; a supply that is renewed daily as God forgives your sin.

Question #106: *What do we pray for in the sixth petition?*

Answer: *In the sixth petition, which is, "And lead us not into temptation, but deliver us from evil," we pray, that God would either keep us from being tempted to sin, or support and deliver us when we are tempted.*

No Christian can ever dare approach the Holy God who is our Father without praying, *Forgive us our debts*. However, no Christian should ever be content to leave it at that but should also pray, *Lead us not into temptation but deliver us from evil*. In the former petition, we confess our sins and ask forgiveness. In the latter, we confess our weakness and ask for help and protection. These two requests naturally follow in perfect order.

If you have experienced true repentance, if you have confessed your sin to God and received forgiveness, then you have a holy dread of falling into sin again and grieving your Savior. You remember what it cost Him to forgive you and thus wish to live a life pleasing to Him. So you pray, *Lead us not into temptation.*

This has been called a prayer for the early morning. We have so many temptations of every kind facing us every day. There are temptations of the mind as well as the body. There are so many situations filled with temptation. You have to deal with people every day who tempt you to compromise your principles and deny your Lord. Surely, every day should begin with this prayer.

This is also a prayer for the early morning years of life. Every child, every youth, should have this prayer constantly on his lips and on his heart. The older you grow, the more you will understand the urgency of this request. The bird with the broken wing may fly again, but not with the same freedom or to the same soaring heights. So we may be forgiven by God's grace, but sin may still weaken and lessen our freedom and our influence for good. Of course, this prayer should not be limited to the early morning hours of the day or the early morning hours of life. Even the very old have need of this prayer every day.

This is one of the most important and urgent requests we can ever make known to God. In this prayer we ask that we may not have to face dangerous temptations. We ask our Father that we may not be led astray by our own ignorance or willingness. Far too often we wait far too late to ask for help. The time to think about the depth of the water is before we dive in and discover we cannot swim. It is foolish to put your head in the lion's mouth and then pray that he not be hungry. So temptation should be studiously and prayerfully avoided. In this petition we ask that, when overtaken by temptation, we may not fall. God allows us great freedom, and under His providence we may be tempted. Job is a classic case in point. God did not tempt or afflict Job, but He allowed him to be tempted. When we are tempted, this petition asks that we may be given the wisdom to see sin for what it is and the power to resist it.

Basically, this is a prayer for a closer walk with Him who was tempted and tried at all points as we are, yet without sin. No one has ever faced the severity of temptation as Jesus faced it. No one has ever won greater victory.

Finally, when we pray this prayer, we ask God that when we are tempted and when we do fall, that we may not be enslaved by the evil one. *Dear Lord, when I fall victim to temptation and sin, do not allow it to become a way of life with me. Do not let me, your child, become a servant of Satan. When I am hurt, do not let me become bitter or resentful. When I see hurt and suffering all around me, do not let me become callous or careless. If I win some spiritual victory, deliver me from self-righteousness. When I am too busy to pray, don't let me think I didn't really miss very much.*

Question #107: *What doth the conclusion of the Lord's prayer teach us?*

Answer: *The conclusion of the Lord's prayer, which is, "For thine is the kingdom, and the power, and the glory, for ever, Amen," teacheth us, to take our encouragement in prayer from God only, and in our prayers to praise him, ascribing kingdom, power, and glory to him, and in testimony of our desire and assurance to be heard, we say, "Amen."*

The Lord's Prayer ends where it began, in heaven. It ends with the same concerns with which it began, the glory and the kingdom of God. All that is said before in this prayer awaits these final words. It is incomplete without this final ascription of faith and praise. Because we can pray these last in faith and confident hope, we are assured all the requests of this prayer are answered. If in our prayers we are always seeking the kingdom and the glory of God, there is no question about the answer. John Calvin said these words are given us that we might be reminded again our prayers are grounded altogether on the goodness and power of God and not upon ourselves. The maturity of our Christian experience may be measured not so much by the length of our prayers, but rather by the amount of praise and worship we include in our prayers.

At last we come to the final words of the Lord's Prayer. They form a grand finale, a capstone of faith and prayer, *for thine is the kingdom and the power and the glory forever.* What a daring thing to be able to say these words. Only the eye of faith can see it in this troubled world. Only the voice of faith can proclaim it. By these words we declare our faith in God and His Word.

When the Apostle Paul was speaking to the men on the sinking ship which was bearing him as a prisoner to Rome, He encouraged them with these words: *Sirs, be of good cheer for I believe God.* If there were ever a time when this testimony is needed, it is now. People are fearful and anxious. The world is in so much trouble and despair. How cheering it is to hear the voice of faith saying, *Sirs, be of good cheer for I believe God.*

In these final words, we are saying to God, *Father we are sure of you, you are trustworthy.* To the world we are saying, *God is in control and therefore we have hope.* The kingdom of God may be veiled and invisible now, but it is a real kingdom and will one day burst forth to be seen by all. *The kingdoms of this world will become the kingdoms of our Lord and of His Christ, and He shall reign for ever and ever.* This prayer is an act of dedication and commitment. When we pray these words, we are making a personal commitment to God and His kingdom. When we say, *thine is the kingdom,* we have no mental reservations. We acknowledge our part in that kingdom and our responsibility to it.

Praying these words is like taking your life and placing it in the hands of your heavenly Father to use as He pleases. When you say these words in prayer, you are crowning the Lord Jesus Christ as your personal King and Lord. This is an act of dedication that is final and irrevocable.

Finally, this prayer raises life's most important question. The word *forever* implies the question, *Where will you spend that forever?* You will never face a more urgent and relevant question than this.

You may say these words every day, *thine is the kingdom and the power and the glory forever*, but it takes more than just saying the words to ensure a place in that grand forever. There is only one way, and that is the way of faith in God's Son. It is putting your faith in the Lord Jesus Christ as your personal Savior. When you have made that commitment, you have entered the forever kingdom. Amen.

www.ingramcontent.com/pod-product-compliance
Lightning Source LLC
Chambersburg PA
CBHW050111170426
43198CB00014B/2533